No Thanks to Mom and Dad

Emma Jean Meyer

outskirts
press

Outskirts Press, Inc.
http://www.outskirtspress.com

Paperback ISBN: 978-1-9772-1876-6
Hardback ISBN: 978-1-9772-2295-4

Library of Congress Control Number: 2020900538

Outskirts Press and the "OP" logo are trademarks belonging to Outskirts Press, Inc.

PRINTED IN THE UNITED STATES OF AMERICA

This book is dedicated to my beloved husband.
Without whose support and encouragement,
I could never have finished this story.

Table of Contents

PREFACE

It was the summer of 1933. The country was in the grip of the Great Depression. The young father, with his twin girls at his side, stood looking up at the huge brick building sitting high on the hill. He stared intently at the sign which read St. Vincent's Orphanage. With a heavy heart, he grasped a tiny hand in each of his and began to walk up the gravel path. It was a long walk for the two year old girls so he walked slowly, bent over in order to hold their hands. He grieved that he was unable to provide for them. How would all this end, he wondered.

The long walk was tiring for the youngsters. They began to fuss and stopped often to play in the gravel. The big house on the hill was intimidating and they begged to go home. As they approached the top of the hill, the driveway was lined with bright colored flowers. The twins rushed to pick them but were quickly recalled by their father. As they looked up, there, right in front of them was the big house. They looked to their father for reassurance, but found instead, a broken man with tears in his eyes.

Wan and Em sat quietly beside their father. The parlor was dark and ominous to the little girls. The nun, in her strange attire, fascinated them, but all this was dwarfed by the sorrow they felt for Daddy. Why would he not stop crying? What did the strange lady say to him?

Eventually, their father rose to leave. The twins sprang to their feet. Now we can leave and Daddy will feel better, they thought. Their father hugged each of them fiercely and went out the door. As the door closed behind him, they screamed "Wait, Daddy, wait for us." They pushed on the big door and cried hysterically. The nun tried to comfort them but they continued to cry and call for their father. As they watched him disappear down the long pathway, they realized he was gone. They wept quietly in total resignation.

CHAPTER I

Since we were only two years old, Wan and I were taken to the nursery. We were bathed in tubs that stood on high legs. After the bath, we were covered with a brown salve to kill the lice and Scabies. During the bath, I impulsively reached out and gently slapped the nun who was bathing me. Sister Mary responded with a slap and a warning not to do that again. The burning in my cheek re-enforced her admonishment. I certainly would not do that again.

After the bath we were left to play with the other children. All of the children in the nursery were under the age of six. An older girl and sister Mary took care of them. We had our own little dining room with tiny metal tables and metal high-chairs. The children were seated four to a table with the older girl seated at her own table. It was cozy and quiet and we felt comfortable there.

Breakfast always consisted of oatmeal mush and milk. Try as I might, I couldn't bear to eat the mush. It was full of hulls and barely warm. On more than one occasion, I was left alone at the table till I finished it. With all the other children gone, I was fearful and tried valiantly to finish it.

Sometimes my sister, Wan would eat the mush for me and other times I gave it to the other children. Finally, in desperation, I poured it behind the steam radiator, which provided heat for the dining room. I sat in my chair quietly, dreading the wrath of the nun and hoping she wouldn't find the mess behind the radiator. I repeated this episode every day till I left the nursery.

When we reached the age of six, we moved up to the "little girls" dorm. All the girls in the "little dorm" were six to eleven years old. This worked out well as the big girls were too big for them and the nursery girls were too small. The "little dorm" was a huge room with five or six beds placed end to end. In one corner was the nun's room which was divided off with curtains, which were kept closed.

The bathroom contained three bathtubs, six basins, and four stalls. At the end of each bed was a wooden box with a lid where the girls kept their belongings and their treasures. Each girl was assigned a number which was put on everything she owned. It was on her clothing, inside her shoes, and on the wooden box. Wan was number 97 and I was 98.

Just as in the nursery, the older girls helped take care of the younger ones. They bathed them, combed their hair, and helped them with their chores. Wan and I were excited to move up at the orphanage. We were learning our identity and setting goals for ourselves. We were called "The Gabby Twins" by the older

The Gabby Twins, 1936

girls but this didn't bother us. We had plenty to say.

Our day began with the Daily Mass. This was followed by breakfast in the dining room. This room accommodated all the girls in the orphanage with the exception of the nursery. For breakfast we were served oatmeal mush (again), bread and butter, and sorghum molasses. Many battles were fought over the extra bread and some resorted to hiding it in their clothes. Although we wanted the extra bread, we were too proud to resort to hiding it so we did without.

When breakfast was finished the older girls washed the dishes and the younger ones swept the floor. After school, we were free to play.

We had a nice playground with swings and teeter totters, and lots of trees for hide and seek. One of our favorite activities was taking old paint cans and making stilts. We took gallon size paint cans and turned them upside down. By feeding string through the holes in the sides, we were able to tie them to our feet and walk in them. Many skinned knees later we were quite proficient at walking in our homemade stilts.

We also made our dream homes in the dirt with long winding driveways outlined with pebbles. Another pastime was finding a tiny hole in the ground. We learned that if we took a long blade of grass and placed it in the hole, before long it would start to wiggle. By withdrawing it ever so slowly and carefully, you could bring up the blade of grass with a large insect still attached.

Other girls took June bugs and tied a string to one of their legs. By holding the end of the string, the bug would fly like a kite. While toys were scarce indeed, there was no shortage of entertainment. What one girl didn't think of, the other did.

Occasionally, we were treated to a free movie, coupled with a cartoon. I still remember how I felt when I first saw Pinocchio. With eyes wide in wonder, I swore never to tell another lie. After the movie was over, we trudged the three blocks back to the orphanage. We discussed Pinocchio's nose and wondered whether this could really happen.

The cliffs were a special place for the girls to play. The residing Pastor, after much begging and pleading, would carefully lead the girls over the cliffs. On the backside were long pathways of erosion. The yellow path, so named because of the yellow color of the dirt, was our favorite. We would seat ourselves at the top of the hill and slide down as far as we could. One after another, we slid down the hill, screaming with delight. One day one of the girls tripped and fell over the cliffs. We never knew how badly she was hurt. They took her away and we never saw her again. This misfortune ended our trips down the cliffs.

Another great delight for us was joining the Girl Scouts. Each Monday evening, the Scout leaders came and held meetings and taught crafts. In the Fall came Girl Scout cookie time. This presented us with our first taste of freedom. We were allowed to go down the public streets for a specified distance to sell the cookies.

Proudly dressed in our uniforms, Wan and I set out to show the world who we were and what we were selling. When we finished, we walked back to the orphanage feeling both pleased and tired. On one such occasion, one of the girls got into a car with a stranger. She was never heard from again and the Girl Scout program was eliminated. Despite our efforts, we never learned what happened to her.

Visiting days at the orphanage were the second and fourth Sundays of each month. The children looked forward to these days with wild excitement. Daddy was faithful about coming each visiting day. Wan and I knew if we swung real high in the swings we could see over the top of the hill and watch the visitors come up the long path. Sure enough, we saw our father each Sunday. His confident stride was easy for us to recognize, and our hearts leapt with joy.

In August of each year, we were allowed to spend two days with our family. Two whole days with Daddy all to ourselves was almost more than we could imagine. Sometimes he took us to the amusement park where we had picnics. The best part for me was that wonderful peanut butter and crackers. While Daddy and his friend, Evelyn, visited, we were off to ride the rides. Daddy gave us a whole handful of nickels to ride anything we wanted. When the nickels were gone, we came back for more, but he told us there was no more. Oh, well, there was still that wonderful peanut butter.

At other times on these special days, our Uncle George and Aunt Hettie came for us in a big black car. We sat in the back seat feeling very special indeed. Uncle George, in his straw hat, with his blue eyes flashing, would tease us and laugh loudly. Aunt Hettie would look back at us and smile warmly. Then they would ask us if we remembered who they were. With beaming smiles, we responded "You're Uncle George and Aunt Hettie."

Wan (left), Emma (right)

Little did they know how much happiness they had brought to two little girls. They took us to their house where we played with their children. Then Daddy would come, and with him playing the violin, we sang songs till it was bedtime. It was a wonderful two days.

As we grew older, each child was assigned duties in the laundry room. While the laundry was done by a hired woman, the ironing was done by the girls in order for them to learn. There was a large coal stove at one end of the room where the irons were heated. They were held with hot pads and were very heavy. Although our little hands could hardly hold them, we learned to iron despite many scorches on the fabric and painful burns on little hands.

While every day seemed the same, special days such as Christmas and Easter found the children wildly exuberant. As Christmas approached, we wrote our letters to Santa Claus. We were allowed to ask for three gifts. We were told to put the most important gift first on the list, followed by two other requests. With all the things we wanted, how could we possibly pick out three?

On Christmas morning, we filed into the recreation room to see Santa. Gifts were piled high on huge tables and there, beside them stood Santa. As each girl's name was called, she went forward to receive her gifts. Their smiles were radiant. The next week was spent in wild delirium as we played with our toys and compared gifts.

It wasn't long before we were approached by the nuns to give up two of our gifts for children needier than we were. If each girl gave up two gifts it would make a nice donation for the missions. How, we thought, could anyone be needier than we were? Sadly, and with great reluctance, we surrendered our new gifts.

Easter was special too. All the board members came and a giant Easter egg hunt was held on the front lawn. Again, Wan and I were too proud and foolish to join the hunt. To our chagrin, the girls were allowed to keep the eggs they found.

Another important day was the annual Orphans' picnic held on the Fourth of July each year. This event was highly publicized and the attendance from the public was enormous. Early in the Spring, booths were set up in the back yard which was high on a cliff. We watched the workers string wires for the outside lights on the booths. We could hardly wait for the big day to arrive.

Rudy, 15 years old, Bill, 13 years old, Twins, 11 years old, June 7, 1942

If your family came to the picnic and could give you any money, you were free to spend it any way you wished. There were grab bags, toys, rides, and lovely baskets of fruit done up in yellow cellophane. I was fascinated by the fruit baskets and placed my dime on a number printed on the counter. If the wheel stopped on your number you won the basket of fruit. After losing two dimes, I was ready to move on, but excitement drove me back and I placed one more dime on the counter. This time they called my number. I had won! I kept calling out that I had won but no one could hear me above the noise of the crowd. When they called the next number, I knew my basket was gone.

Choking back the tears, I went to find Wan and Daddy. I knew just where to find him. He was always standing at the beer booth with lots of other men and Wan was there with him. Daddy was proud of his twins and took every opportunity to show us off. Being musically inclined, we were able to harmonize, and this pleased him. After singing a song for him, we were off looking for more excitement. Soon the day ended and the public left. The next day we cleaned up the trash from the picnic and were allowed to keep any money we found. We were sad it was over.

The grounds at the orphanage were tended by a janitor who lived in a little house on the property. He was always busy firing the coal furnace and performing other duties.

The trash was taken by the girls to the furnace room for the janitor to burn. One day the children were no longer allowed to go to the furnace room. I was delighted as I intensely disliked the janitor. He chewed tobacco, his teeth were yellow, and his grin was evil. Before long the word was out. One of the girls had been raped. We were too young to know what this meant, but it was obvious to us that it was something bad. The janitor left and the young girl was sent to a home for "bad girls."

One night the children were rudely awakened and roused out of bed. During the night the orphanage had caught fire. As we filed past the enormous hole in the floor, our imaginations ran wild. Wan, upon seeing the firemen in their yellow suits and strange hats, was totally convinced that Hitler had come to get us. Although we were too young to understand the war, we knew the name Hitler was something to fear.

I, meanwhile, was completely preoccupied with my drop-seat pajamas. The elastic was sprung in the drop-seat which allowed my backside to be exposed. How could I ever get past those men? I couldn't let them see me. With one hand holding my pajamas tightly shut, Wan and I filed past the big hole in the floor, our eyes wide with fear.

As we passed through the big hall, I saw my Daddy standing next to the Grandfather clock and he was crying. Eagerly, I ran toward him but was quickly pulled back into line. Why was Daddy crying? Where was Wan? Suddenly I felt panic. Wan was always beside me.

Unknown to me, my twin sister, in sheer terror, had hidden in a small closet in the dining room. This was a safe place away from all the confusion. As she hid in the closet, Wan watched as the firemen ran past, calling her name. As each one went by, she huddled deeper in the closet, trembling in fear.

She watched as a cockroach ran up and down the closet wall.

As the roach approached her, she burst out of the closet, right into the arms of a fireman. As he grabbed her, she fainted, completely terrorized. The last thing she heard was "I've got her." The fireman wrapped Wan in a blanket and carried her to a waiting bus. The girls were taken to a nearby orphanage till the necessary repairs were made.

After the fire, life returned to normal. The older girls taught the smaller girls everything they could. Clothes were passed down from child to child as were shoes and coats. Our coat consisted of a pullover sweatshirt with our number printed on the inside. Most often when we went to get it, it was gone, so we simply took the one next to it or stayed indoors.

The used shoes were kept in a little room called the shoe closet. When we needed shoes, we got the key and went to get them. It was a real adventure to find a shoe you liked that had a mate, and even more exciting was finding a pair that fit. Of course, finding matching pairs for twins was nearly impossible, but searching for them was pure pleasure for both of us.

As we grew older, we learned a different side of life.

Spanking by Sister Mary was not unfamiliar to us, but we were totally unprepared for what was in front of us. Sister Superior had a rubber paddle with corrugations on one side which she used unmercifully. Many times, the whippings were cruelly undeserved.

In a rage, she would grab one of the children and whip them with the rubber paddle. In sheer desperation, the girls banded together and stole the paddle from her office. In mortal fear, they threw it over the cliffs as far as their little arms would allow. The entire group of girls were called to the office and questioned. Only by sticking together did we prevent her from learning who did it. This painful episode is indelibly etched in our minds and will never be erased.

Around the age of eight, we met our mother for the first time. Although we were excited, we were apprehensive as well. What was she like? Would she like us? It wasn't a regular visiting day when she came, but having come a good distance, we were permitted to see her. She was an attractive woman, slender of build, with brown hair and eyes. A strange man was with her who we later learned was her husband. We sang songs for her and tried hard to impress her, but she was distant and cold, so we gave up trying. As I remember, she didn't stay long. Before leaving, she told us that the nuns had chastised her for "living in sin" and as a result she would not return. Although we didn't understand, we accepted her explanation with indifference. Every year while we were at the orphanage, she sent us a large box of goodies at Christmas time. Inside was candy, cookies, raisins, and hair ribbons. Childlike, we were thrilled without ever giving a thought to Mom. As one might imagine, the goodies didn't last long with so many reaching hands.

We never saw Mom again until about the age of sixteen. I can't remember ever receiving a letter from her and even worse, I can't recall even thinking of her. With all the children to play with, our days were full and there wasn't room for this woman called Mom.

The disappointment of meeting Mom was tempered by the frequent and joyous visits of our father. He laughed a lot and

Bill & Rudy Milam

played with us. He sat us on his knees and called us "Snookums." His visits were the highlight of our lives. We waited eagerly for the second and fourth Sundays of each month and we were seldom disappointed.

Around this time, we learned we had two older brothers who were in an orphanage for boys in the same town. On special occasions we were taken to the boy's orphanage for visits with our brothers. Since we saw them so seldom, we couldn't remember their faces, so we waited patiently for them to find us. When they finally found us we hugged each other fiercely. To us, these two skinny boys were like gods. They were our brothers!

On one occasion Wan was suffering with diarrhea. In desperation, she asked her eldest brother to take her to the restroom. Since the boy's restroom was off limits to the girls, he protested, saying he would get in trouble. When she pleaded with him, he bravely stood in front of the door, blocking any of the boys from entering. This simple act only re-enforced their bond.

It was customary for the girls around the age of ten to learn to cook and sew. Each girl took her turn peeling potatoes and making breakfast. At first it was new and exciting, but we soon looked upon it as drudgery. Every morning there were the admonitions not to break the yolks of the eggs and the sizzling bacon burned our arms. The sharp paring knife inevitably cut our fingers and it was impossible to hide the blood from the nun. It seemed we just couldn't do anything right.

The smell of the bacon brought out the worst in us twins. After the meal was cooked, it was sent up on a dumb waiter to the nun's dining room. We stole a piece of bacon off the tray and sent it down to the basement to be retrieved later. We wallowed in the taste without ever a thought of the dirt and grime it had laid in.

We also learned to embroider and made batches of lye soap which were cut into squares. The lye soap was melted down and used for washing clothes as well as bathing. Our reward for these efforts was a good grade on our report card.

From cooking we moved on to sewing. The sewing room contained many sewing machines, and large bolts of cloth. We made our own underwear, slips, and dresses. We mended tears, and darned socks. We were beginning to feel a real sense of accomplishment. We were learning so many things.

We had moved up to the "big girl's" dorm and were now part of the "big girls." We were looked upon with respect by the younger girls. We were given special privileges by the nuns. Some were assigned to ring the dinner bell, while others did special chores, such as going after the mail. The Post Office was several blocks away so this was really special. The fun in ringing the dinner bell was riding the rope from floor to ceiling repeatedly.

We were about eleven when we made our first dresses. It was a difficult task as everything had to fit just right. After much ripping, the dresses were ready to be hemmed. Feeling my individuality, I decided to hem my dress a little shorter than the approved length. When I put it on, I happily bragged how much better it looked than the longer dress on my sister.

Dresses too short

Wan, although she agreed, warned me that I would get into trouble and asked me to change it. No sooner had she spoken than Sister burst into the room in a rage. In sheer desperation, I began to defend myself as best I could. The two of us struggled and I was cut with the scissors. I re-hemmed the dress to the proper length and told myself right then and there that I would leave and not come back. I not only was cut and bruised, I was humiliated in front of all the girls. After convincing Wan to go with me, we went through the ranks till we found someone who had a dime to ride the city bus. Clad in the same dresses, we waited till dark to leave.

Whether it was luck or Divine intervention is uncertain, but somehow, we found our way to Daddy's house. We knocked on his door and waited eagerly for him to open it. When he saw us, instead of being overjoyed at seeing us, he was angry and gruff. His first words to us were "Now, look what you've done. You'll end up in the home for bad girls." Wan and I looked at each other in dismay. We had never seen Daddy like this. He pulled us into the house until the authorities came to take us back. We were returned to the orphanage in disgrace.

In time all this was forgotten. We were approaching the eighth grade, the time for leaving the orphanage. Our brothers had graduated and gone to live with Daddy. We asked Daddy often if he would take us as he had taken the boys and his reply was always yes, so we accepted this and were happy in the knowledge that soon we would be a real family. Fate, however, was about to deliver the cruelest blow of all. In the summer of the next year, we were twelve years old. That same year Daddy married Evelyn. She was the same lady who went with us to the amusement park when we were younger. She too, had girls at the orphanage. This fact made little impression on us. There was plenty of room for two more and we could be a big, happy family.

Then one day reality hit us. Daddy and Evelyn were taking her girls home to live with them but since there wasn't room for all of us, we were being left behind. We waited and prayed for Daddy to come and get us but he never came and he never explained why. He began coming less often to see us and we soon realized that Daddy had gone with his new family and we weren't part of it.

In June, 1945 we graduated from the eighth grade. As graduation was held in the evening, we spent the entire day preparing for it. We cleaned and decorated the chapel. We ironed our pretty dresses and borrowed from each other anything that would complement our appearance. We swapped shoes, hair ribbons, and any jewelry we could find.

Sister Matthew, who was in charge, was not very well liked by the girls. We tolerated her presence and ignored her suggestions. We were too excited to be bothered. When the entire class was ready to dress, Sister Matthew took each girl and rolled her hair in curlers and combed and set it for her. We marveled as she worked miracles with our hair. Here was a side of Sister we hadn't seen before. Maybe we were wrong about her. After a full day of work, she was ready to help us look our best. She kept working till the girls, all seven of us, looked totally different.

We learned a valuable lesson that day. We wondered whether we had ever really given her a chance to be kind to us.

We were sad at the thought, but excitement overtook us and we continued our wild preparations. After the ceremony was completed, we retired to bed, exhausted, but elated. We had finished school and were ready for anything.

Where we would go from here never entered our minds. This was home, what else was there? One day that summer, we were taken upstairs to pack our belongings, and put in a car. A heavy-set woman accompanied by a nun drove us away. As we sat in the rear of the car, Wan and I wondered where we were being taken. What in the world had we done? There was no talking and no explanation was offered. We sat silently, each one lost in her own thoughts.

Upon entering the brick building, we were greeted by a matronly nun who hugged us and asked if we remembered her. As it turned out, this nun was the one in charge when we were first taken to the orphanage. As she wiped away the tears, she told us how she had laid all night with her arms outstretched with one of us on each arm. Although her arms ached, she wouldn't move for fear of waking us and the incessant crying would start again. She told how we called for Daddy and would not be comforted. We stared at her in disbelief. Although we couldn't remember her, we knew we had found a friend, someone who truly cared. This bond would last to her dying day.

Chapter II

Owensboro was a sleepy little town about 100 miles from Louisville. Sister Francis had requested that we be placed in her care when we left the orphanage. She was Superior of a co-ed High School which boarded no more than four needy children. There were the two of us and two older girls living there. In return for our lodging and education, we worked in the kitchen and laundry and any place else that we were needed.

One duty that I particularly enjoyed was getting in the milk. It was delivered by a horse drawn milk wagon in tall glass milk bottles which the milkman left on the porch. Being a horse lover, I watched eagerly each day for the milk to come. Before I retrieved the bottles, I always visited with the horse. He was white, with a soft pink nose. I somehow managed to find a carrot or apple for him to eat each day. As he chewed, I talked to him and rubbed his soft nose. I think, in time, he began to watch for me as eagerly as I watched for him.

Sister Francis was kind and patient with us, but at the same time, she kept a safe distance between herself and us.

Although we knew she loved us, we never felt free to talk openly with her. She showed her love for us in many ways. She never went shopping that she didn't bring something back for us. One of the gifts that I can still remember was a little pill-box hat that she bought for us. It was brown and very smart looking. We always wore it to church on Sunday and as we walked the five blocks to church, we felt very special.

Another gift that I can vividly remember is what she gave us for our fifteenth birthday. She took Wan and me to the local beauty shop for our first perm. our hair was naturally curly, so we didn't really want a perm, but rather than hurt her feelings, we accepted her gift. We watched in wonder as the beautician curled our hair in rollers that hung from long electrical cords attached to a large bonnet. We were instructed to tell them if any of the curlers got too hot. As I remember, it seems they all got too hot and the big bonnet was most uncomfortable. Several hours later, when we looked in the mirror, we were shocked and dismayed. I felt tears come to my eyes as I looked at Wan. Her shoulder length hair was cut short above her ears. My wavy hair had been replaced with tight little ringlets all over my head. We never let Sister Francis know how disappointed we were.

Although Sister Francis was good to us, she was also a stern task master. We understood that she expected the best from us, not only in school, but in everyday life as well. On more than one occasion, she sternly reminded us that we were to obey the rules or we would be gone. These words struck terror in our hearts. Where in the world would we go? Who would take us? It was clear to both of us that we would obey the rules.

One summer morning, we rose early as we always did. Wan was complaining of pain in her right side and had a temper-ature. The Doctor had said it was appendicitis and surgery was needed promptly. Owensboro didn't have a hospital so she would have to be taken to Louisville. Sister tried to reach Daddy in Louisville as his permission was needed for surgery, but she was unable to locate him. Afraid to wait any longer, Sister Francis hired an ambulance and she and Wan left for Louisville, leaving me behind.

Two or three days later, I went with one of the nuns to see Wan in the hospital. She was in a lot of pain and my heart ached for her. I joked with her and made her laugh, not real-izing that laughing only caused her more pain. Evelyn, our new step-mother, and her two girls who had been in the orphanage with us were there also and I was filled with resentment. Why did they have to intrude on my only day with Wan? But I said nothing. Soon Wan came back to school and things returned to normal. Because of her stitches, she was relieved of her daily chores, (mine doubled) and I can still see her going up the three flights of stairs backwards to keep from pulling on her incision.

The teen years were a new and pleasant experience for Wan and me. We were assigned daily chores, but when they were completed, we were free to do as we pleased. Many Sunday afternoons we walked to the local theater to see the movie. In those days there was always a double feature playing and of course, they always saved the best film for last. Since it was

Wan & Me about 16 yrs.

a double feature, we felt we really got our money's worth. We were expected to start supper about four o'clock, so, as a result, we rarely got to see the ending of the feature film. I can still remember sitting there at the movie till the very last minute desperately hoping to see the ending. Finally, when we knew we could wait no longer, we left. As we walked home, we discussed how we thought it would end. Although we were disappointed, it was a small price to pay for our new found freedom.

On other days, we would dress up in our long broom stick skirts and high heels and walk aimlessly all over town. Broom stick skirts were the rage at that time, and clad in ours, we felt just as big as any other teenager. Although the high heels hurt our feet, we walked block after block, knowing that the whole world was looking at us. Wan would smile at me, and I, at her, and we'd say to ourselves, "Look, world, we're the Milam twins." Finally, we would return to school and reality.

While we were at the orphanage, we were given piano lessons which we really enjoyed, but now, we were learning to play other instruments. Wan began playing the violin and I played the flute. Daddy had given Wan his violin, so she was able to play anytime she wished. I would accompany her on the piano and much to the nuns' dismay, we rocked the walls with our music. We played Blues and Jazz till we were finally asked to quiet down. I've wondered many times in my later life, how the nuns survived not just one of us, but two! Just as at the orphanage, what one twin didn't think of, the other did.

In the four years we were at Owensboro, I can't recall Daddy coming to see us over four or five times. His wife, Evelyn, had family in Owensboro, so she visited with them while Daddy visited with us. On special occasions, he took us over to her family's house to spend the day. Although we didn't know them, they made us feel welcome and we enjoyed ourselves. But the best part for us was when Daddy spent the entire day with us at school. Daddy played the violin and Wan and I both accompanied him on the piano. The walls reverberated as we played for hours. Daddy loved country music and he could tear at your heart strings with his rendition of "The Orange Blossom Special". To this day, it brings tears to my eyes every time I hear it. They are tears of joy as well as sadness.

In 1948, I was in my third year of High School. President Harry S. Truman was touring the country by train during his run for a second term. His train was scheduled to stop in Owensboro where he would make a short speech. Since we were taking a course in Political Science, Wan and I were allowed to go to the train station to see him. Much to our delight, he stepped out on the platform of the train where everyone could see him, and gave a short speech. Although it didn't last long, we proudly felt that we had just taken part in the history of our country.

In January of the following year, Mr. Truman gave his Inaugural Address. I listened with my ears and my heart. When he had finished, I sat down and wrote him a letter, saying how much I enjoyed his Inaugural Address. Months later, much to my surprise, I received a letter from President Truman thanking me for my letter and asking for my prayers. I can't begin to tell you how I felt. To think that President Truman had responded to my letter was beyond my wildest dreams.

In the afternoon after school, as we cleaned the numerous classrooms, the walls echoed with the sounds of a young, female voice. It was a lovely voice, strong and vibrant. Wan and I listened as she went up the scale and down the scale, practicing till it was perfect. Father Saffer, the Guidance Counsellor, recognized her talent, and coached her endlessly. As she sang the songs from the current musicals, he advised her and challenged her till he brought out the best in her. Soon she was filling the halls with her rendition of "Oklahoma", which sent goosebumps down the both of us. Who was this person with the charming voice?

When we could stand it no longer, we opened the door to see, pretending that we needed something from that room. To our surprise, there she was, Florence Henderson. She was two grades behind us in school. Although we knew who she was, we never paid any attention to the younger girls. We were the Juniors, they were just kids. Father Saffer showed his displeasure at being interrupted, so we quickly exited. Florence was sent to New York when she finished High School where she occasionally sang on Broadway and TV, and eventually starred in her own TV series, "The Brady Bunch".

As graduation was approaching, Wan and I decided that we needed to have a job in order to pay for class rings and sweaters. Sister had told us early on that she would provide for us whatever we needed, but no extras. We applied for work at the local dime store and were accepted. We bravely went down to the Social Security Office and got our Social Security cards. We worked every Friday and Saturday for fifty cents an hour. We saved our money diligently and enjoyed the freedom our job afforded us. We saved enough money to take our class trip, pay for our class rings and sweaters, and most importantly, our graduation. We met other girls our own age, and best of all, we learned about boys.

Until now, boys were only pests, and something we just had to tolerate. They were always teasing us and hiding our books from us. They seemed to like Wan and me, but they were always getting us into trouble. Can you see me going up to the chalk board with only one shoe? Those awful boys had thrown one of my shoes out the window, and sure enough, I got called to the blackboard. Rather than tell on them, I told the nun I didn't know what happened to my shoe. Here I was, in trouble again!

Before long, I began to see boys in a different light. Although they were a real pain, they could also be very charming. What in the world was happening? Soon, Mr. Special came along. His name was Billy Joe, and he had the most intense blue eyes I had ever seen. And guess what! He wanted to take me roller skating. My heart was pounding and my self-esteem had gone through the roof. Someone thought I was special! Wan, too, had a boyfriend, and the four of us went roller skating every Saturday afternoon, and then to the Drive-In theater on Saturday night. Life was really looking good and we loved it.

I guess every set of twins has done this, but we had lots of fun confusing our dates. We'd switch off, with Wan taking my date, and I, hers. Sometimes we'd go through the entire evening without the boys realizing what we had done. But other times, we'd see them studying us and we knew we had to come clean. Then again, we'd be talking and forget which one we were and the cat was out of the bag. As a rule, the boys were good

Wan & Me about 17 yrs

natured and put up with our games. All this stopped, however; when Billy Joe entered my life. He was my first boyfriend and I wasn't sharing him with anyone, not even Wan. Besides, she had her own friend, Earl.

It is with sadness that I write this part of my story. I am sad for the hurt we caused by our thoughtlessness. Another one of our duties at school was preparing the meals for the pastor. He would come to the school for his meals and return home when he was finished. The usual procedure was to place the newspaper at the side of the table along with a pack of cigarettes and matches. One day we decided to light up one of the cigarettes to see what they were like. Wan and I took a puff or two and discarded it. From then on, we would smoke whenever we felt like it just because we could.

Finally, one day, Sister Francis called us to her office. To this day I don't know how she found out, but she scolded us severely. The hurt look on her face broke our hearts as she told us how disappointed she was in us and that she wondered if drinking would be next. With heavy hearts, we assured her that it would never happen. I will never forget the hurt we caused her, that wonderful person, who loved us so much. That night, Wan and I promised each other that we would never, ever, do anything to hurt her again.

In the spring of each year, the school would have music recitals. This gave the music students a chance to perform for their families and loved ones. It was a big affair, with the girls dressed in formals and the boys wearing suits. Since Wan and I didn't have a formal, one of the other nuns made us one. It was a soft pink dotted swiss with a long rose-colored sash. It had big puffy sleeves and the sash fell all the way to the floor. We were delighted with them, but we never got to say thank you because we never knew who had made them.

Daddy never came to any of our recitals. Over time, we had lost touch with each other, so we never invited him. But we could always count on our eldest brother, Rudy. We always invited him and we always knew he'd be there for us. He and his wife would drive to Owensboro from Louisville and go back the same night just for us. Our dear brother, Rudy, was still the only father figure in our young lives. We never realized how much we asked of him, and he always gave of himself, willingly and generously. I remember one recital when Wan and I played a duet on the piano. It was a lively piece which the audience loved. They gave us a standing round of applause and right there in the middle of it was our brother, Rudy. What a guy!

The following summer, we learned Rudy was living in Evansville, Ind. He had found work there after leaving the military at the end of the war. He came to Owensboro to see us often since Evansville was only an hour away. Upon learning that Mom was living in Evansville, we begged Rudy to bring her with him the next time he came. One Sunday afternoon we got a big surprise. Rudy had come in his little red Oldsmobile to see us and had brought Mom with him. We hugged and talked with Rudy, and then turned to Mom. She hugged us lightly, and took a seat in the swing on the back porch. Rudy visited and played with us for about three hours, while Mom remained seated in the swing the entire time. She never talked with us, asked about our lives, or appeared interested in any way. I can still remember my feelings of bewilderment. I studied her and tried to understand her. Mom left with Rudy and I never saw or heard from her again for about three years.

It was customary in those days for the Juniors to take the Seniors on a class trip. Wan and I and the rest of the Junior class took them to Notre Dame College and campus. While we were fascinated with the huge dome and the school, the best part was the guys on the football team. They were courteous and friendly and we were ecstatic. We had shaken hands with the Notre Dame football team!

For a literary assignment, all the students were told to write an essay about the trip and the best essay would be presented to the Bishop and the whole school. To my surprise, my essay was chosen to be presented. I don't think I was ever so nervous in my whole life. I memorized my essay and with trembling hands and voice, I recited it. Later, Wan and the nuns complimented me, but I was only glad it was over. It was after this that I began to take some interest in writing. I entered many essay contests and tried writing poetry. I never won any contests, but I received great satisfaction from writing.

Throughout our teen years in Owensboro, we lost touch with our second brother, Bill. He was a young married man with a family to care for, and we just never heard from him. We wrote him letters but he was too busy to respond, and in those days, you just didn't phone each other as they do today. But our thoughts were always of our two wonderful brothers and dear Daddy who we never saw any more.

As spring approached, the Seniors were busy making plans for the prom. It wasn't as lavish an affair in those days as it is today. It was the big band era, so dance halls were everywhere. We piled as many as possible into cars and met at the local dance hall, which was appropriately named "The Frolic". It was a favorite teen spot on the edge of Owensboro. There was no live band and no chaperones that we knew of. We waltzed to the jukebox which played the tunes of the big bands, and jitterbugged in our formals. our lovely dotted swiss gowns swirled with each movement as we danced and sang along to our favorite songs. After the banquet was finished, we said our goodbyes and headed home to Sister Francis, who was waiting up for us. She listened patiently as we rambled on and on about the prom and our wonderful evening.

Soon, it was June, and time for graduation. We were fitted for caps and gowns. We practiced for choir, and learned how to walk in the processional to the music of Pomp and Circumstance. we had our class rings, and class sweaters and had taken our class trip. It was an exciting time for both of us. As the big day approached, we called again on dear Rudy. Who else would share our excitement? Daddy was too busy with his new wife and we knew he wouldn't come. That evening dressed in our white caps and gowns, and white high heels that hurt our feet, we started the long walk down the armory aisle. Wild with excitement, we scanned the crowd for Rudy. Sure enough, there he was, smiling at us. I can't tell you the feelings I felt for Rudy that night. I wanted to laugh and cry at the same time. That dear young man who was both daddy and big brother did, indeed, love us and we knew it. The tears come to my eyes as I write this, remembering the love and joy I felt that day.

It wasn't long before Sister Francis approached Wan and me about where we would go from here. We had finished High School and were ready to move on with our lives. I can still remember her exact words to us. She said "Where do you want to go from here? We are finished with you." I trembled as I felt my heart go clear down to my toes. We had never given a thought to anything changing in our lives. In fact, leaving the nuns and being on our own was the farthest thing from our minds. Finally, Sister suggested that we could take a job at a hospital, run by the nuns in Lexington Kentucky. We agreed, and at that moment we both realized that we would soon be on our own, responsible for ourselves, and making our own decisions. With mixed feelings, we packed our bags, and with the nun accompanying us, we boarded the train for Lexington. I can't remember saying goodbye to Sister Francis or anyone else. It was at this time that Sister Francis dropped out of our lives, but not our hearts.

CHAPTER III

The ride to Lexington was quiet and uneventful. The gentle rocking of the train made us drowsy and we dozed peacefully, forgetting our feelings of apprehension. Upon arriving, we gathered up our luggage and started the long walk to the station. As we struggled with our bags, porters in black uniforms and red caps took them from us and hurriedly carried them to the station. We stared at them and thought to ourselves how kind they were. Only when the nun tipped them generously did we realize they were being paid for their services.

As we walked past the train, it would periodically emit great bursts of steam which frightened me. No one else seemed to even notice it, but I was sure I would be burned if I got too close. Afraid to ask the nun, and more afraid of being burned, I carefully dodged each burst. I was relieved when the long walk was over and we entered the station.

When we arrived at St. Joseph Hospital, we were taken to the office to meet Sister James who would look after us. She was a younger nun and quite pleasant. She led us through a long tunnel which came out in the nurse's building. This is where the student nurses lived while they went to nursing school. We were assigned a room, all to ourselves, just for us. It contained two twin beds, two dressers, and our own private bathroom. We would be responsible for cleaning it and linens would be furnished by the school. We were overjoyed to say the least. We decorated it as best we could, with what we had. We couldn't believe our good fortune.

Next we were taken over to the hospital and introduced to the nursing staff. We would be working for fifty cents an hour as nurse's aides in assigned areas. We toured the hospital in total awe. We were seeing things we had never seen before. We saw sick children and adults with incisions across their throats. We saw traction devices and people with broken limbs.

In those days, the male patients were separated from the female patients in different wings of the hospital. When we toured the men's ward, we were frightened. We had never been around men and we were intimidated by them. But Sister told us we would to have taken our turn working in the men's ward as well as the other wards. Feeling sick inside, we accepted her words, knowing we were going to learn many things, some good and some not so good.

Sister James gave us some uniforms and bought us a pair of white shoes for our first day of work. We worked five days a week, rotating from one place to another in order to learn our duties. Wan and I were separated but on the same floor. We looked on the doctors with awe and managed to dodge them most of the time.

Finally, one day my luck ran out. One of the doctors cornered me and asked me to help him with something. He asked me a question which I couldn't answer. Without even responding, I turned and ran. I hid in the bathroom, quaking in fear till I thought he was gone. From then on, I ran every time I saw a doctor approaching. There were never any repercussions from this, and eventually, I was able to overcome my fear and learned to respect and admire them.

After about a month at Lexington, Sister James came to me and told me Wan was leaving and going into the Convent to become a nun. She would be leaving right away and we should say our goodbyes. I was so shocked at what I heard I felt no emotion whatsoever. Thinking back, I was so stunned that I didn't even realize that Wan was leaving me. We hugged each other tightly and in minutes she was gone. I worked my shift that day in a daze. Later that night when I went to bed, I cried myself to sleep, realizing my twin was gone. Who would share my secrets? Who would share my joy and my hurt? For the first time in my life I was alone and afraid.

In the Fall, the nuns offered to put me through nursing school which I gratefully accepted. My new roommate was starting school also and we got along very well. My schedule was very full and left little time for fun. I attended class in the mornings and worked in the evenings as an aide. School supplies were given to me but the extras such as soap, shampoo, and clothing were left up to me.

I liked nursing school and was making good grades, but the

loneliness I felt was overwhelming. Christmas came and went with no family to share it with. The other girls were kind to me and bought me gifts, but I longed for my precious sister and my brothers. Every free weekend I boarded the bus for Nazareth to see Wan at the Convent. I was greeted warmly by the nuns, but Wan later told me that I should stop coming so often. It was against the rules for her to see me so much. But I was undaunted. I continued seeing her every chance I could. In retrospect, I wonder if anything could have stopped me.

After spending an hour or so with Wan, I went to Louisville, where I spent the weekend with my brother, Bill. His young wife made me feel welcome and we shared lots of good times together. Rudy was living in Indiana so I didn't see him much anymore, but I had lots of lost time to make up with Bill. Sometimes, when he was able, he would take me back to Lexington, stretching our time together as far as he could.

I remember one trip I made when Bill insisted on taking me home. Although I had a bus ticket, he wanted me to go back with him. A friend of his offered to drive us back, but Bill and I would have to ride in the rumble seat. Afraid that I would be offended, Bill asked me if I minded riding in the rumble seat. Did I mind? I would have walked to Lexington if it meant being with my brother. I joyfully told him no and I set out on one of the greatest trips I ever made. Although the bugs stung your face and the night air was cool, it was a time I will always treasure. There we were, Brother Bill and I snuggled together in the rumble seat, talking and laughing, oblivious to the rest of the world.

One Saturday morning, the house mother called my room to

tell me I had a visitor. As I never had visitors, I told her she must be mistaken. She insisted there was a young man to see me and I should come down. Confident she was mistaken, I went downstairs. There stood a young man in a military uniform. I didn't recognize him at first, but when he told me who he was, I nearly fainted.

Jimmy was a boy at the boy's orphanage whom I liked when I was in the eighth grade. Although it was against the rules, we had our boyfriends. We sneaked letters back and forth and bragged about it. We rarely saw each other, but everyone knew Jimmy was mine and I was his. Upon leaving the orphanage, Jimmy was completely forgotten.

Now he was going overseas on military duty and he wanted to see me before he left. We spent the day together, talking of old times. Before he left, he asked me to marry him so he would have something to hold on to. I was tempted to say yes out of sympathy for him, but my good sense told me no, you can't build a marriage on sympathy so I declined. I have thought of that moment many times and thanked my guardian angel for nudging me.

I was doing quite well in my schooling. I liked nursing very much and was adapting well. I overcame my fear of doctors and admired and respected them. I even learned to like working in the men's ward. They were friendly and easier to please than the women.

I learned Sister Francis had been transferred from Owensboro, to Louisville where she was in charge at St. Mary and Elizabeth Hospital. We corresponded often and I sent her every test paper, good and bad. She encouraged me and advised me. How I wished she could have been there with me.

I received my nurse's cap and was as proud as I could be. I was finally going to be somebody. In a few more months I would finish my first year of school and receive a blue band on my cap. I learned to give injections and practiced faithfully on oranges while the teacher supervised. There was so much to learn I thought my brain would explode.

The school had a smoking lounge where everyone went to smoke. It was the only place where smoking was allowed. I soon learned if you wanted to be part of the crowd you gathered in the lounge and you smoked. It was a fun place to be. We told jokes, laughed, and sang songs. The smoke was so thick it burned your eyes.

Before long I began to smoke, and soon I was part of the crowd. We went to the corner drug store and sat for hours, smoking and listening to the juke box and drinking soda. At that time, the most popular song was Vaughn Monroe's "Racing With The Moon". We played it over and over. What a voice! When the owner finally ran us off, we returned to the smoker for more singing and smoking. I never had the funds to buy my own cigarettes but there was always someone willing to share. All the girls were kind to me, loaning me their clothes, and paying my way to the movies.

In spite of their kindness, my heart was empty and I ached for Wan. I traveled nearly every weekend to see her and my brother Bill. Rudy and I were corresponding and he often told me if things got too bad I could always come and live with him.

I never heard from Dad although I did visit with him occasionally for short periods of time. I never felt wanted by Evelyn, his wife, so I kept the visits brief.

In time the loneliness became unbearable. Rudy's invitation to come live with him echoed in my mind and I debated which I wanted more, nursing or my family. Childlike, I never thought of my future. I could only think of all the love I was missing and how badly I wanted it. However, if I went to Indiana with Rudy I would be farther away from my sister. I finally decided if Rudy would take me to live with him, I could work and travel to see Wan.

I talked to Sister James and told her of my decision. She gave me my money which I had given her to keep for me and I bought my bus ticket to Evansville, Ind. Rudy met me at the station and took me to his home. They had a two year old son I was crazy about. He had big dimples in his cheeks that got even bigger when he smiled. I got a job at the local drug store which was about a mile away. I walked to and from work every day, happy as I could be. I had a job, my family, and best of all, a home.

My mother was living in Evansville at that time also. She was married for the third time and often asked me to come stay with her. I didn't like her husband very much, but I was eager to get to know her. She and her husband didn't get along very well. There were many fights over my being there. He was always civil to me, but many nights I laid awake listening to them argue over me. Mom always defended me but I felt guilty for being there and causing problems. I began to alternate staying with her and then Rudy. When I felt like I was becoming a burden I would go and stay with the other for a while. While this was hard, it kept peace in the family.

Mom was always good to me, but try as we might, we simply couldn't get close. We went shopping together and we confided in each other, but somehow, there was always a gap between us. When we hugged, it was not a mother-daughter hug, it was more like a hug between friends. I talked to her as I would a friend, without any feelings of love or respect. I have to wonder if we weren't both afraid. Afraid of rejection, afraid of hurt, and afraid to love. How truly sad for both of us.

I continued my trips to Kentucky to see Wan and Bill every chance I got. Having a full-time job, I wasn't free to go any time I chose. Bill came occasionally to see Rudy and me and I cherished every visit. Soon I came to realize I was seeing less and less of my twin. Although this was painful, I realized I had to accept it.

One day there was a knock on the door. When I opened it, I was surprised to see Michael, a boy who I had gone to High School with in Owensboro. I had dated him occasionally, but had forgotten him when I left. Somehow, he had tracked me down and wanted to resume our friendship. I didn't really want to date him but he insisted so I began to go out with him. We had many good times together, but before long he began to get serious, and spoke of marriage. I suggested that we break it off and I never saw or heard from him again.

Late one evening around seven o'clock, a young man came to see Rudy. They worked together and he needed to talk to him. As he entered the apartment, the electricity went off leaving us in darkness. While Rudy lit some candles, I joked with the young man, saying he was the reason the lights went out. Soon the lights came back on and the magic began. When I saw him my heart began to pound and I felt like it would burst. Here stood the young man of my dreams. As I stared at him, my heart sang, and I knew, I knew.

With trembling heart and hands, I began to talk with him. I learned his name was Richard. He had soft blonde hair and striking blue eyes. Before he left that evening, he invited me to go to the Merry-Go-Round with him on the following Friday. Without hesitation, I told him yes. As I waited impatiently for Friday to come, I began to wonder what I had done. What was the Merry-Go-Round? Was it a club, a restaurant, a motel? I felt panic as I struggled with myself, trying to decide what to do. Knowing I had to make a decision, I approached Rudy.

Neither he nor his wife ever heard of the place. After much debate within myself, I decided to risk it. I murmured a prayer and decided come what may, I was going to the Merry-Go-Round with Richard. I would take my chances and deal with whatever came.

When Richard came on Friday evening, I was dressed in my Sunday best. I only had two good outfits, so what I would wear was no problem. As we departed, I asked him what the Merry-Go-Round was. I chose my words carefully so as not to offend him. Knowing I was new to Evansville, he told me it was a restaurant where all the teens gathered. After dinner we drove around for a while and eventually parked on the street so we could talk. In no time at all, we were told to move on by a local policeman. As he took me home, I began to realize I was crazy about this wonderful guy, this country boy with the soft voice, who I had only just met.

We continued seeing each other every chance we could. Since I was still going back and forth from Mom to Rudy he never knew where to look for me. His family didn't have a phone, nor did Mom or Rudy so we had no way to communicate with each other. But every Friday I got all dressed up, confident Richard would be there. He never disappointed me and our relationship grew.

It wasn't long before Richard proposed to me. Although I told him I wanted to think about it, I knew what the answer would be. I was taught that by stalling you wouldn't appear too eager. Before the evening was over, I knew I could contain myself no longer. With a joyous heart, I told him I would marry him and spend the rest of my life with him. I promised myself at that moment, that with God's help, I would make my Richard happy no matter what the cost. I dared to dream of having a family, a home, and the two of us growing old together.

We set the wedding date for September 12, 1950. That was on a Friday night, our magical night. Rudy and Blanche had moved back to Louisville, but they agreed to be our bridesmaid and best man. I worked all the overtime I could get in order to buy clothes and flowers for the wedding.

I found a lovely satin, knee length dress. It was a soft green with tiny ruffles on the neck and sleeves. I chose the green to complement Richard's suit, which was a brown pin stripe. It looked handsome on him and flattered his masculine build. I decided to have yellow roses for the bridal bouquet and boutonniere.

I bought a brown alligator purse with alligator shoes to match. Although funds were short, I was determined we would look our best.

I ordered the flowers from a florist who frequented the drug store where I worked. We chatted when she came in and we soon became friends. She made up a lovely, small bouquet and brought it to me at work the day before our wedding. I still have our wedding flowers. I pressed and dried them, and now, forty-nine years later, I still have them.

I found a small furnished apartment for us, and with Richard's approval, I moved in. It was only three small rooms with a bath. The rent was fifty dollars a month and no hot water. I heated all the water for cooking, and washed our clothing elsewhere. We were allowed to take a bath once a week and no more. On Saturday the landlord would turn on the hot water heater. She waited till evening to turn it on so we could use it only for baths, and then it was turned off till the next Saturday. The landlord lived in the front of the house. She was a widow trying to make ends meet, who was all alone except for her tenants. We told ourselves we would find something better as soon as we could. Before long, Mom, who had become divorced, moved in with me. We thought we could help each other by sharing expenses.

About three weeks before our wedding, Rich and I made a trip to Nazareth Convent to see Wan. I wanted her to meet him and get to know him. As we talked, she told us how unhappy she was and that she wanted to leave but had no place to go. As her letters were censored, she wasn't free to write about it. Before I could utter a word, my beloved Richard told her not to stay if she was unhappy. She could come and live with us anytime she was ready.

The next week we received a letter from Wan saying she was leaving the Convent and could we pick her up. When we arrived the next day, the Nuns told us she had already gone. We returned to Louisville and immediately went to Rudy's house. Wan was there with him and his family.

Upon questioning, she told us that unable to take it any longer, she had taken the bus to Louisville and gone to Dad's house. Upon her arrival, Evelyn pointed her finger at Wan and loudly informed Dad that "she can't stay here." Without any objections, Dad arose, took Wan by the hand, and led her out the door. He offered no explanation or apology. He didn't even tell her where he was taking her. This frightened and bewildered girl didn't even have a pair of shoes on her feet. She was wearing a moccasin type slipper which the nuns used as bedroom slippers.

It was a long walk to Rudy's house. Wan asked herself why this was happening. As they walked, where was Daddy taking her and why could she not stay with him? She fought back the tears as she struggled to keep up with him. When they arrived at Rudy's house, Dad talked with him and asked him if he would take her.

Rich and I visited a short time with Rudy and then headed back home taking Wan with us. The anger I felt toward Daddy was dimmed by the joy I felt. My sister was going home with me. My dear Richard was at my side, and the three of us were going home. We were going to be a family.

Richard and I were married the following Friday. It was a simple wedding, held in the rectory as he was a Protestant and I, a Catholic. My friends from work were there as well as Wan. Rudy and Blanche stood up with us as we had planned. We returned home that night and went to work the next day. Our honeymoon would have to come later.

Several months later, the landlord informed Richard that there were too many of us living in the apartment. She would tolerate three people but not four. My heart sank to my toes as I realized I would have to ask one of them to go. I agonized over what to do. Mom, at least had a job and income, Wan had nothing. There was absolutely no way I could ask Wan to leave. It would have to be Mom.

I approached her and told her of my dilemma. She immediately became offended, and protested, saying she was paying her own way. I explained how Wan couldn't leave without even a job and that it was she who had to go. Mom left, still angry with me. We didn't see or hear from each other for a long time.

Soon Wan found a job. She had also begun dating. It wasn't long before she became engaged and we were preparing for another wedding. She was married in December. It was a big wedding, held in the church. She asked me to be her bridesmaid, but I declined. Being newlyweds, we didn't have the money for a gown. I watched with pride as she walked down the aisle. No one in our family was there except Richard and me. There was a big dinner afterward which we attended and then we left for home. The inevitable was happening. Wan and I were going our separate ways.

One day Richard came home from work and told me he had been laid off at Chrysler. It seemed like every time we turned around there was another layoff. Till you acquired some seniority, you were among the first to go. Most of the time the layoffs were short lived, but occasionally they lasted for several months. We learned to save money for those times and managed to survive them.

This one however, lasted quite a long time. Unable to find work and with our funds depleted, we put our few belongings in the car and set out for Louisville. Surely, we could find work there and maybe Bill or Rudy would know where to find something.

We had bought a little 1940 Plymouth convertible. It was a deep green and very attractive. We were very happy with it except for one problem. It ran like a jewel but if you shut off the engine it was impossible to restart. The only way to make it start was to put it in gear and pop the clutch. We avoided shutting off the engine as much as possible, but when it was unavoidable, we knew Richard had to push while I started it. While it was a problem, we were young and strong and we lived with it.

Upon arriving in Louisville, we found a small furnished apartment on Eastern Parkway. Rich found work at a furnace company and I went to work at Walgreens. Rudy and Bill came to see us often. It was wonderful having the family so close to us. Many times, on my day off, I would go see Dad at his place of work. He was a maintenance man at the government housing complex so I could visit as long and as often as I wished. Dad was always glad to see me and we had many long talks together.

One thing that Dad really worried about was Wan having gone to the Convent. He always thought that she became a nun because of him. I'm not sure why he felt that way, but he agonized over it and questioned me many times. Somehow, he felt he was to blame. On one particular occasion I remember, he placed his head in my lap and cried. He kept asking over and over "Was it because of me?" It broke my heart to see Daddy cry, but I couldn't answer his question.

I never knew why Wan became a nun. I never asked her and we never discussed it. To this day I don't know. I have to assume that she thought this was what she wanted, or perhaps the nuns persuaded her. As long as we were around them, I can remember them trying to recruit all the children.

———◆———

Before long Rich got laid off at the furnace company. Work was slow so he and many others lost their jobs. We gathered up our belongings and headed back to Evansville. In time he was recalled to Chrysler and our life returned to normal.

Richard and I found a little house in the country that was renting for $12.00 per month. It had no running water, no sink, and no bathroom. It was a three room, shotgun type house. We put a coal stove in each room to keep us warm. The stripper pits were only about seven or eight miles away and putting a trailer behind the car, we would go dig our own coal and bring it home. A trailer load would last about a month and then we'd go dig for more.

Rich built me a sink for the kitchen. As there was no drain, I caught the water in a bucket and emptied it when necessary. The well was just outside the back door. I filled a bucket with water in the morning and carried it inside and put it on the sink. I put a dipper in the bucket to be used for drinking. I used a kerosene stove for cooking which I came to like very much. If it was turned up too high it would black up the stew pans and smell terrible. But if used properly, it did a fine job and was very economical.

I dreaded the trips to the outhouse. It was cold in the winter and in the summer, there was always the bees and the snakes to contend with. I remember one occasion when I was sitting there and a large snake crawled out right in front of me. Needless to say, I came out of there with my clothes around my ankles for the whole world to see. I would postpone going as long as I could, but eventually, the dreaded trip would have to be made. While we didn't have everything the way we liked, we could save money and someday we would buy a house of our own.

We were only about two miles from Richard's Mom and Dad. We had a good relationship with them and saw them often. Every Monday I took our laundry over to her house and she and I washed together. It was an all-day job, using a gasoline powered washing machine. We hung the clothes on the line to dry and much later in the day we finished.

Richard was the oldest child in the family. There were four other children ranging in age from two to twelve years. The children loved to come to our house and they stayed overnight many times. We had a TV which we all enjoyed watching. Many

Friday nights they stayed with us and watched TV while their Mom and Dad went out.

Rudy and Blanche came to see us occasionally and Bill and Ruth came also. Bill had a young son named Rusty about six years old, who came with them. He was so full of energy he became bored quickly. The house was just a few feet off the highway so he couldn't play outside. We had a good size back yard which bordered a railroad track, so we were afraid to let him play there also. It kept the four of us hopping just to keep up with him.

One day we received a letter from Dad and Evelyn saying they were coming to see us the following weekend. I was thrilled that Dad was coming but I was uneasy about seeing Evelyn. I cleaned the house thoroughly and went to the grocery. I wanted everything to be perfect. I tried hard to plan good meals for them on our limited budget.

Remember, we had no plumbing and no running water.

I was making a salad at the kitchen table while Evelyn sat there talking. When I proceeded to slice tomatoes to put in the salad, she informed me that she didn't like tomatoes in the salad. Upon hearing this, I became enraged and attacked the tomatoes with a vengeance. For the first time in my life I was in control and I intended to take full advantage of it. I deliberately loaded the salad with extra tomatoes.

Evelyn had a deep, irritating voice which grated on my nerves. I don't think Dad ever realized how I felt about her. If he did, he never showed it. I truly despised her but I kept it to myself.

We drove them around town and tried to show them a good time. Even in the car, Evelyn talked incessantly in her deep monotone voice. Finally, the weekend was over, and they left for Wan's house. I was sorry to see Dad go, but I also had a sense of relief. As far as I can remember, that was the only time Dad ever came to our house.

I don't remember how things went at Wan's house. The only thing I remember is Wan telling us how Evelyn ridiculed our house. She laughed because we had no running water, and grumbled at having to use the outhouse. Although it hurt, I pushed it out of my mind. I was always told you have to crawl before you walk, so I thought of this time as our crawling time. Richard and I were happy and that's all that mattered.

Life was good in our little country house. Richard continued his on again and off again job at Chrysler. Despite this, we knew we were lucky. Right across the highway was a truck body shop. Rich had worked there many times in earlier days. In fact, that's where he and Rudy were working when we met each other. Whenever he lost his job at Chrysler, he could find work right across the street. Although the pay wasn't as good, it was work and we were grateful.

There was a grocery store just down the street so I could walk to get the things I needed. When supplies got too low, we went to Evansville to restock. Rich came home for lunch every day and I eagerly waited for his coming.

Many times, I would tell him before he left for work that I was going over to spend the day with his mother and that I would return before he got home from work. It was a two mile walk so I took my time and walked all the way. She always seemed glad to see me.

I was crazy about my Mother-in-law. She was a pretty woman, a proud woman. She had coal black hair with a white streak running right through the middle of it. You never saw her without her earrings and her lipstick. We hit if off right away. In fact, her first words to me were that she was glad I smoked. Her husband disapproved of her smoking and chided her often about it. Now there were two of us and we both smoked. From that day on, we were friends and buddies.

Since we were living in the country, we didn't see very much of Wan. Neither of us had phones at that time, few people did. It was too far for us to see each other very often. Whenever Rich and I went to Evansville for anything, we stopped by to see her. When Rich was working at Chrysler, I would sometimes ride in with him and spend the day with Wan. Sometimes I kept the car and we would go shopping. We never tired of being together and always looked forward to our next visit.

One day Wan told me she had some wonderful news that she wanted to share with me. She announced that she was pregnant and expected the baby in November. I was delighted for her but at the same time I wished it were me. Soon we were shopping for baby clothes and picking out names. I couldn't wait to tell Richard the news. Before long, we would be an aunt and uncle.

CHAPTER IV

Richard and I had lived in the little country house for a year now. Spring had arrived and with it came more dreams and new adventures. We had bought a used washer and refrigerator and were slowly but surely furnishing our house.

Before long it was May and we received the most exciting news of our lifetime. We were expecting a baby in February. Now, Wan and I were both pregnant and making plans for motherhood. We shopped together for baby clothes and spent hours going over lists of names. We chuckled as we came to realize that we had married three months apart and now we were having babies three months apart as well.

Richard and I were excited at the thought of parenthood. Although it was overwhelming, we were elated and set about learning all we could about parenting. Richard's mom made baby afghans and painted the spare room and decorated it.

Having four sons and only one daughter, she was desperately

hoping for a girl. She made a bassinet covered with white lace and trimmed it with pink bows. At least once a week I walked the two miles to her house to ensure I got sufficient exercise.

During my pregnancy, I occasionally visited with Mom. We talked often of my family and I began to learn about them. Grandma Hardesty and Mom's siblings were still living in the country in Kentucky. The more I learned about them, the more I hungered to know them.

One day, Richard and I persuaded Mom to go to the country with us. I wrote to Uncle Earl, Mom's brother, and told him we were coming. We needed Mom to go with us as the roads in the country were poorly marked and we were afraid of getting lost.

Mom, Rich, and I set out for Kentucky early one Saturday morning. It was only about two hours away so it wasn't a big trip. Mom was lost in her own thoughts and talked little as we drove. Her graying hair blew in the wind as she dozed. Her tiny frame would sway with each turn of the car and her brown eyes would flash as she awoke and chided Richard for going too fast.

My heart was pounding as I realized I was returning to my roots. I was going to meet family that I knew I had, but had never seen. Would they remember me? Would they accept me? I couldn't imagine that they wouldn't love me, they were my family.

Mom knew the way and we never missed a turn. When we reached Cannelton, Ind. we boarded the ferry to cross the

Ohio River into Hawesville, Ky. There was no bridge across the river at that time, so if you wished to cross you had to take the ferry.

After reaching the Kentucky side or the river, we found ourselves in beautiful hill country. The road went uphill and downhill, and after a dizzying ride through the hills, we dropped down into river bottom land.

Before long, we were approaching the dam at Stephensport, Kentucky. Upon arriving, we sat for a while and watched the boats pass through the locks. There was a quiet picnic area on the bank which was inviting but we decided to drive on.

In no time we were entering Kentucky farmland. We marveled at the beauty of the country side. It was Spring and the trees were ablaze with color. The cattle grazed peacefully in the fields while the younger ones raced around flaunting their youthful energy.

As we traveled down the road, Mom would say "Your uncle lives here or your cousin lives here." When we turned on Uncle Earl's road, she told Richard to stop the car. As we looked around, she told us we were looking at the house where Wan and I were born.

It was a tiny house, which appeared to be only two rooms. She told me how she and Dad and Rudy and Bill lived there during the Depression years. The landlord gave them free rent as they couldn't afford to pay anything.

When we were born the landlord gave them the use of a milk

cow so they would have milk for us children. She told us how she stuffed mud and paper in the cracks of the house, trying to keep out the cold. Every morning our diapers would be frozen on us because the wood stove was unable to heat the house.

She told of putting us on the horse as she and Rudy and Bill walked down to the creek to wash the clothes. While Bill, the younger, played in the creek, it was Rudy's responsibility to watch us girls. She said Rudy stayed at our side faithfully and entertained us while she did the wash in the creek.

On one of these occasions, Mom had taken her pet pig along with us. It was a small pig which intrigued my brother, Bill. As Mom did the wash, and Rudy watched us, Bill slipped off and went up on the bridge. When the opportunity was right, he dropped a large rock onto the pig, killing it. Mom said she was heartbroken over this event. I'm confident Bill didn't realize what he had done.

Later, when I discussed these things with my brothers, Rudy told me how he remembered walking to school every day barefoot. When he left home, Mom instructed him to remove his shoes and carry them. Upon arriving at the school, he would wash his feet in a puddle and put them back on before entering. They were only allowed one pair of shoes a year so they had to last.

We continued down the road for several miles. As we approached the next house, Mom said her sister, Beulah lived there. We asked her if she wanted to stop and see her but she said no. Next, she showed us where her mother was living, and then where her brother lived. She still declined to stop.

Soon we arrived at Uncle Earl's house. He greeted us warmly and I immediately liked him. He was a tall slender man with dark hair. His skin was tanned and leathery, and his features projected the Cherokee Indian in his ancestry. He had a large nose and dark brown eyes which seemed to look right through you. His back was slightly stooped as if the years had taken their toll.

Although they had a large family, they made us feel welcome. We visited late into the night, talking and reminiscing. It was clear to me that Uncle Earl and Mom had a special relationship.

Early the next morning, we went to see Mom's other brother, Joe. He was more talkative than Uncle Earl and a lot of fun. He had a lovely wife and three daughters. He also had a horse named Charlie that I was eager to ride, but being pregnant, I decided it would be better if I didn't.

Before long, there was a knock on the door. Uncle Joe called to me and Mom to come see who was there. It was Grandma Hardesty. It was nearly a quarter-mile from her house to Joe's and this dear lady walked all the way to see us. Grandma was a short woman as I remember. Her hair was gray and her eyes, even when she smiled, were sad and withdrawn. She carried herself in a proud but tired fashion. She wore an apron over her cotton dress which she tugged at continuously. It was obvious that life had been hard for Grandma. Mom introduced Richard and me and then she and Grandma went outside to talk.

I can't recall much emotion between Mom and Grandma. They hugged each other, but there was a strained, tense feeling that was obvious. I studied Grandma and watched her as they talked. There was a sadness about her and she seldom smiled. My heart was heavy as I looked at her and thought of the many moments, those grandma / grandchild moments that we never had. How sad that we were never able to enjoy them. Richard took a picture of the three of us, Grandma, Mom and me which I will always treasure.

As we left for home, I asked Mom again as we approached her sister's house if she would like to stop and visit. She told me no, that she and Beulah hadn't spoken to each other for years. Beulah had scolded her for leaving us years ago and she didn't want to hear any more of it. She said if we wanted to visit, we could just let her out and she would walk. Rather than do that, we went on past, but I decided I would see Beulah on my next visit.

I wondered if there had been words between Mom and Grandma. To this day I don't know, I never had the courage to ask her. I feel in my heart that something happened between them and their love for each other was smothered by bad feelings. I can't even imagine the terrible hurt that Grandma must have felt.

I was only vaguely aware of the trip home. My thoughts were of my family, my Mom and Grandma. I was very impressed with both of my uncles. They were warm and friendly and I was happy to know them. Dear Grandma made me feel sad and happy at the same time. I was happy to finally meet her and I wanted to learn more about her. At the same time, she made me feel sad because she appeared so unhappy. She smiled ever so lightly when she smiled as if to say it's not allowed. I wondered what kind of burden she was carrying. Had she and Mom had words?

Next I thought of Mom. I remembered how she and Grandma had hugged each other, not warmly, or lovingly, but stiffly. While Mom hadn't been to the country in many years, she didn't seem excited about returning, or seeing her family. I remembered that we didn't stop at Grandma's house, but rather, went right on to Earl's. I was confident that something had come between them and deep in my heart, I felt it had to do with us children. I hoped the day would come when I would learn more about it.

My thoughts returned to Mom and Dad. I wondered what life was like for them in that tiny house. The Depression was in its darkest days, work was scarce, and they had four little children. How frightening it must have been for them, not only to have small children to provide for, but to be so young themselves. They were only twenty-three and twenty-five.

Emma, Wanna & Grandma Hardesty

Will Milam & Celestine

As I pondered these things, I felt an overwhelming sense of sorrow. I realized that love was not only wonderful, it was painful as well. I knew I would return to the country and my family. There was much I needed to learn about them.

In no time at all summer was gone and winter was upon us. Wan had a little baby girl in early November. She named her Christine and she was the joy of our lives. While we enjoyed her tremendously, our thoughts were always of the child which we were expecting in February. The days seemed to drag on and on.

As it was a mild winter, I continued my daily walks. Richard was working fairly steady and things were looking pretty good for us. I bought a used crib for the baby which I refinished and now it was a matter of simply waiting.

On Feb. 21, 1952, Connie made her debut into the world. She was only five and one-half pounds, but she had a fine set of lungs and she wasn't afraid to flaunt them. She voiced her op-position at being born and received our undivided attention. In no time at all, I realized life was certainly going to be different.

Richard's mom asked us to stay with her for a few days which I gratefully agreed to. Elated at having a granddaughter, she had put pink bows on the curtains and all around the room. Connie was the star of the show and she loved it. She would gurgle with delight and bellow her disapproval in a matter of seconds. Grandma fussed over her continuously as I watched in won-der. This precious gift from God was certainly going to change things.

When Connie was four months old, I realized I was pregnant again. This couldn't have happened at a worse time. Richard was laid off at Chrysler again, and unable to pay our own insur-ance, we had let it expire. How could we possibly pay a hospital bill and provide for another child?

We saved every nickel we could for nine months, and when little Jerry came, we were able to pay the hospital bill and doc-tor bill as well. Jerry made his appearance on March 21, 1953, exactly thirteen months to the day after his sister. No one was prouder than Richard and I. While we were frightened at having two small children, I made up my mind that somehow, some way, we would provide for these children not only the necessary things, but the **love and stability of a home. I was determined to give them what I never had.**

Before long I began to think of the country again and my fam-ily there. I hungered to know more about them. Grandma Hardesty and I wrote letters to each other and I occasionally corresponded with my uncles. After talking with Wan, we decided to drive over to see them. She and her husband would follow us in their car since they didn't know the way. We decided to split up, with Wan and Dick staying with Uncle Joe while Rich and I stayed with Uncle Earl. They lived right next door to each other on adjoining farms.

Early Saturday morning we decided we would ride Charlie, the horse. Uncle Earl went to the pasture and brought him to the barn. Rich offered to ride him first as he expected him to be unruly after the long winter vacation.

Uncle Earl warned Richard that the saddle and bridle were old and had hung in the barn for years. The ground was extremely soft and muddy. Richard mounted Charlie and away he went. As Charlie ran, his hooves dug deep into the earth and the mud flew behind him.

As Richard turned him around to return, Charlie spotted the barn. He took a deep breath, dug in his heels, and headed for it. At the same time, the cinch strap broke on the saddle and off came Richard and the saddle while Charlie ran for home. With mud balls flying from his feet, Charlie kept on going while Richard stood there on his head, stuck in the mud, with the saddle dangling between his legs.

He looked so funny standing there on his head that we couldn't stop laughing. Uncle Earl ran to open the barn door so Charlie could get in. Wan's husband, who was a city boy, was standing next to the barn. As Charlie approached in a dead run, Dick, her husband, became frightened of him and jumped the five-foot fence. Since he weighed about 180 pounds, none of which was muscle, it was not only surprising, it was funny.

When we finally stopped laughing, Uncle Earl had Charlie in the barn and Dick had recovered from the high jump. We carried the saddle for Richard while he cleaned his clothes, and returned to the house. He was a muddy mess but he was still laughing.

Later in the day, Grandma Hardesty walked down to Earl's and invited Wan and me to her house for dinner. I don't know what her thoughts were, but the invitation was for us girls only. She told us to be there about five o'clock. I didn't really want to go as we were having so much fun at Earl's. I felt shame at what I was thinking. That dear little lady was my Grandma. How could I possibly feel that way?

Wan and I set out for Grandma's house that evening. We talked as we walked, wondering what it was going to be like. Why did she invite only us? Did she want to talk about Mom and Dad? Were there things she wanted to tell us?

When we arrived, Grandma greeted us at the door. Upon entering, I was surprised to learn there was no electricity. There was a kerosene lamp sitting in the center of the table, while the rest of the house was dark. The walls were covered with pictures of her family. She told us who they were, but not knowing our family, we didn't know of whom she was speaking.

After dinner, the three of us sat out on the porch and talked. There were so many things we wanted to ask her about Mom and Dad. She spoke in a soft, sad voice which matched the sadness in her eyes. She told us how Mom, when she left Dad, had taken us to her house and asked her if she would keep us. She promised to come back for us as soon as she was able.

One day Daddy came to her house, and in a drunken rage, took us away from her. I remember asking Grandma "Why didn't you keep us?" She replied almost in a whisper "How could I? You were his children." Then she started to cry. It broke my heart to see Grandma cry like this and I knew I couldn't continue this conversation.

As I watched her wipe the tears, I understood the sad eyes and the sad smile. Dear Grandma was indeed carrying a heavy burden. Did Mom, perhaps, blame her for letting Dad take us? No matter how badly I wanted answers, I knew I would have to find them elsewhere. I couldn't bear to give Grandma any more pain.

We thanked her for dinner and hugged her tightly. This dear lady had won a place in my heart, a special place that was hers alone. We walked back to Uncle Earl's with mixed feelings. We left the next day for home. Richard was a little sore from his fall from Charlie, but we laughed every time we thought of it.

By this time, we were becoming more adept at parenting. Our tiny babies had become toddlers. Grandma Meyer had made some little print dresses for Connie which looked darling on her. I would starch and iron her little dresses and have her walk across the room. If the dress didn't stand out and bounce when she walked, I took it off and starched and ironed it again. Connie had curly blonde hair and big brown eyes. I was the proudest mom in the whole world.

Jerry was an adorable little boy. He, too, had blonde hair with piercing blue eyes just like his dad. He had big dimples in his cheeks and when he smiled, he tugged at your heart strings. My favorite outfit for him was a pair of pants with "Don't Spank" right in the center of the back. Strangers would stop me as we walked down the street and comment what a pretty little boy I had. My heart was bursting with pride.

One summer day I was busy working around the house when I discovered Connie was gone. I immediately went outside; confident she had run into the street. With my heart in my mouth, I ran up and down the road, calling her name. When I couldn't find her there, I ran back to the railroad track behind the house. By now, I was frantic. I returned to the house, un-sure of what to do.

I checked each room again, but still, no Connie. As I approached the living room, I looked behind the door. There sat Connie in the corner behind the door. She wasn't doing anything except sitting there, looking up at me. I scooped her up in my arms as tears ran down my face. I don't know what possessed her to hide there, but I know I aged ten years that day.

Jerry, too, gave us a scare that summer. He had a bad habit of running around with his tongue stuck out. Whenever he was absorbed in doing something, he would have his tongue stick-ing out, completely pre-occupied with what he was doing. He and Connie were running through the house one day when Jerry tripped and fell. When I heard the screaming, I ran to see what it was about. There stood Jerry, covered in blood, with his tongue nearly bitten in half.

I had never seen anything like this before. As I stared in amazement, I wondered what to do. I finally decided I would take him to the doctor and let him decide. While Jerry screamed hysterically, the old country doctor smiled at me and told me to take him home. Jerry would have to eat ice cream for a long time.

Now wouldn't you think he would love that! He did for a while, but he soon tired of it. I tried everything I could to find variety for him, but before his tongue was healed, he hated ice cream. To this day, Jerry doesn't eat any ice cream.

Before long, the house next to us emptied out. We quickly informed a young couple whom we had known for years. Richard and Paul had gone to school together and he and his wife, Pearl, had double dated with us many times. we had become close friends.

Paul and Pearl took the house and soon they settled in. The two houses were close enough that we could yell back and forth to each other. Paul worked the night shift, as did Richard. As they didn't have any children yet, Pearl would come over and late at night, we'd make pies and visit while the men worked.

On several occasions when we arose in the morning, Connie would be gone from her crib. There was no air-conditioning back then, so I placed her crib next to the window so she would be cool. Pearl would rise early and come over and take Connie out the window to her house so we could sleep late. She was always so thoughtful. We are still friends to this day.

We had been living in our little house for five years now. Our rent had gone from $12.00 to $25.00. Jerry and Connie were now three and four years old, respectively.

We did everything we could to make extra money. We had bought an old panel truck pretty cheap. In the fall, we would load Connie and Jerry in the back of the truck and go to the corn field. We took some toys for them to play with while we gleaned the corn. We parked the truck in the center of the field where we could see it and left them there to play.

We each took a fifty-pound gunny sack and starting at the center of the row, we'd meet at the end. We would drag the sack along the row and pick up the ears of corn left behind by the corn picker.

We worked row after row till we were too tired to go any longer. When we were finished, we had a large pile of corn in the truck which we sold to the local feed mill. I can remember one load which we sold for thirty dollars. While this doesn't sound like much today, at that time it was considered a nice amount. And best of all, our funds were growing. We were beginning to think of buying a home, our home.

We spent much time looking and searching. Soon we found a modest three-bedroom home on five acres of ground. We made an offer to the owners and they accepted it. Our payments would be $55.00 a month. Could we really do this?

We signed the papers and the house became ours. We were excited and frightened all at the same time. I murmured a prayer for us as we went to bed that night. We were going to have our own home. Our crawling time was over, we were learning to walk.

CHAPTER V

In late September, 1956, we moved into our new home. We settled in quickly and set about decorating it. We hung sheets for curtains and made do with what we had. We would eventually furnish it better, but only as we could afford to.

In the Spring, we planted a large garden. I canned the vegetables and served them throughout the winter. We also had several fruit trees large enough to bear fruit. There were apple trees, peach trees and a plum tree. There were also two large grape vines which provided grape juice for jelly. I began to see that we could be fairly self-sufficient with a little planning and effort.

There was a small barn out back which we soon filled with animals. We bought a cow and several calves and of course, a pony for the children and a horse for me. It was quite a job caring for the livestock, but I loved every minute of it.

One day the local feed store was making a special offer. If you purchased 200 pounds of feed, they would give you 100 live baby chicks. They were "straight run" which meant their sex was undetermined. Richard and I talked it over and decided there was room enough for some chickens and we could always use the eggs.

It was a bigger job caring for the little chicks than I realized. I hung a light bulb from the ceiling to keep them warm, and shredded newspaper for bedding. They would huddle around the light and chirp and eat incessantly. The floor was cleaned, and the newspaper was replaced weekly. It was imperative to keep the bedding and feeders clean as the little chicks ate everything in sight, even at times pecking at my rings.

Soon the chicks had grown to frying size. We separated the young roosters from the hens. We would eat the roosters and keep the hens for eggs. Imagine our surprise when we learned we had only 5 hens and 95 roosters! I have to admit I was a bit overwhelmed at the thought of killing and cleaning that many chickens. After giving it some thought, I decided I would kill 10 each week until I finished. When I finally finished, we had a lot of chicken in the freezer, but no one wanted any, least of all me.

In July, my mother-in-law and the kids and I went blackberry picking. There were no bug repellents back then so we doused our ankles and wrists with kerosene, and although it was extremely hot, we wore long sleeve shirts to keep the ticks and chiggers off of us. We picked five-gallon buckets full till we had all we wanted. Hot and tired, we went back home and cleaned and froze the berries. Our freezer was rapidly filling up and we derived much satisfaction from our efforts.

Around Christmas time, Richard's brother, Alan, who was

an avid hunter, gave us a duck which he had killed for our Christmas dinner. Alan had plucked him but had left the cleaning for us. When I cut him open to remove the entrails, I could barely do it. The memories of the roosters came rushing back and I had to force myself to do it. Eventually I finished cleaning the duck and baked it for our Christmas dinner. I was unsure how to cook it so I baked it as you would a turkey.

When it was done, I placed it in the center of the table. It was golden brown and looked quite appetizing. I am told roast duck is a delicacy and quite expensive. Perhaps it is, but I am telling you my roast duck was terrible and none of us could eat it. The meat was dark and very greasy. Although my Christmas dinner was ruined, we enjoyed the rest of the meal. There would be no more roast duck in the Meyer household.

In the Fall of the following year, 1957, we received word that Grandma Hardesty was gravely ill. My dear Grandma, whom I had only recently come to know and love, was slipping away from me. I had become so busy with my family and my new life that I had pushed her into the background. We still corresponded but not nearly as often as before. I knew I had to see her and tell her again how dear she was to me. I prayed I wouldn't be too late.

I called Wan and Mom and invited them to go with me. I asked my mother-in-law to keep Connie and Jerry but she declined saying she had a previous commitment. Richard stayed behind to care for the livestock and since Chrysler allowed no time off except for funerals, he had to work.

The five of us left for Kentucky late in the evening. Wan rode in the back with Connie and Jerry and entertained them while Mom rode in the front with me. I hoped that she would talk to us about Grandma as we drove, but she was quiet, lost in her thoughts.

As we approached the house, Uncle Earl came out to greet us. He told us that Grandma was at Uncle Joe's since they had a smaller family and more room. He parked the car for me as Uncle Joe ushered us in. As I looked around the room, I saw Grandma lying in bed. She looked so frail, so old. I felt the tears come to my eyes as I approached her. I called to her but she made no response. I prayed that she was only sleeping but I knew in my heart it was more than that.

We stayed overnight and decided to leave the next morning. Grandma was comatose and unaware that we had come. I knew my time with her was over and I would treasure forever the time we had together. I would never see those sad eyes again except in the photos that Richard had taken for me.

Wan and I and the children left for home, leaving Mom behind. She wanted to stay with Grandma as long as possible. We talked as we drove about our lives, about how things had happened, and how badly we wanted answers. Would we ever learn the real story? Who would tell us?

When we arrived home, we learned Grandma had passed away. She was buried at St. Theresa's cemetery next to her daughter who had preceded her in death. Wan and I didn't return to Kentucky for the funeral. Grandma was with God in Heaven and she would know how much I grieved for her. She would also know the love I carried for her deep in my heart.

As Richard and I continued with our lives, time slipped away from us. Connie and Jerry were doing well in elementary school, and Richard was working pretty steady.

One day in 1959, much to our surprise, Chrysler announced that they were closing the plant in Evansville and moving to St. Louis. All employees were encouraged to go with them if they wanted to. We were stunned and frightened as we came to realize what it would mean for us. With all those homes on the market, could we sell ours? How would the children feel about moving? What about the livestock? Could we find a home in St. Louis? As we lay in bed at night, we discussed the pros and cons and agonized over what to do. We had nine years with Chrysler Corp. and the pay and benefits were exceptional.

On the other hand, we argued, we were young and ambitious and could probably find work in Evansville. We had made double payments on our home and it was nearly paid for. We could raise our own food and we had our own meat. It didn't seem impossible.

We decided to discuss it with Connie and Jerry. Connie was excited about moving, seeing it as a new adventure. Jerry, however, was adamant about not going. He was a country boy who wanted to stay in the country. We explained to him that there was more than just the big city in Missouri, but he remained unconvinced.

Eventually we made our decision. Chrysler Corp. had announced that as long as those employees who didn't want to go didn't take their severance pay, they would be eligible for rehire. In effect, they could return as new employees but still retain their previous seniority.

This was all we needed to hear. We decided to remain in Evansville and try to make it. If we couldn't find a good job we would move to St. Louis and work for Chrysler again. We felt relief in reaching a decision.

Rich soon found work and life returned to normal. The next several years were quite uneventful. In no time at all the children were in high school. Wan and her family had gone with Chrysler to St. Louis. Although I missed her terribly, I understood it was best for them and their family, which now included 4 children.

We traveled to St. Louis to see them whenever we could and continued seeing my brothers in Kentucky as often as possible. While we were visiting my brothers, I always called Dad to see how he was. Not knowing our way around town, we asked him to come to Rudy's to visit with us. Sometimes he would come, while at other times he declined. Although we were disappointed, we accepted it.

One day Richard and I and Wan decided to go visit Uncle Earl in Kentucky. While there, we stated that we would like to meet our Grandma Milam whom we had never seen.

Katherine, Earl's wife, offered to take us to her house which was just a few miles away. We were very excited at the thought of seeing her for the first time. As we stepped up on her porch, we saw her sitting in the swing with a corn cob pipe in her mouth. Katherine introduced us saying that we were her grandchildren. She turned to us and said hello and immediately looked away.

She was a tiny, frail woman with straight black hair. I never saw her eyes as she looked away too quickly. I waited for the hug that I was sure was coming, but it never came. She didn't invite us in or even ask which of her grandchildren we were. She just stood there on the porch looking off in the distance. Totally confused, the three of us left. We looked to Katherine for answers, but she had none. She was as stunned as we were. We never saw Grandma Milam again. She died in 1959 and we were never told. Perhaps it's just as well. I can only assume that poor Grandma Milam had given all the love she had to give.

One evening in late September, a severe storm blew into our area. Richard was working the evening shift at Bendix leaving the children and me at home. As I watched the trees bending in the wind, I became uneasy. It always frightened me to know that these two youngsters were totally dependent on me when Richard was away from home.

Suddenly I heard a terrible noise. I put the children in the safest place that I could find and rushed to the window. I stared in amazement. Where was the barn? As I peered through the wind and rain, I saw the walls of the barn flying through the air, tearing down fences as they went. I immediately thought of the livestock. Were they gone too?

Unsure of what to do, I called Richard at work. When I told him what had happened, he laughed, thinking that I was joking with him. When I finally convinced him, he said he would be home as soon as possible.

Taking the children with me, I ventured out to the barnyard. Although it had stopped raining, there was still a lot of lightning and thunder which frightened them. I knew I couldn't find the cattle alone and they would have to help me. If they wandered off too far, we would never find them.

When Richard arrived home, we rounded up the cattle and herded them into the garage. Next we gathered up the chickens and the feed that was left. As Connie lifted up her pet hen she laid an egg right in her hand. Of course, this delighted her and she had to show the egg to all of us. Although we were tired and wet, we had to laugh as she proudly displayed the egg.

We kept the animals in the garage until we could build a new barn. With the cold weather approaching, our time was limited, so we started working on it without delay. I never saw a barn go up so quickly. In one month, we had it finished and painted. The children and I finished laying the hayloft floor, while Richard was working. Although we were four tired people, we were proud indeed.

In 1968 fate dealt us another cruel blow. Richard had been working for Bendix-Westinghouse for several years. One day, much to our dismay, the company announced it was closing the plant and moving to Alabama. Again, Richard's job was in jeopardy and we were forced to make a choice. We could go to Alabama or find a new job. We decided it would be best if we returned to Chrysler and moved to St. Louis.

Richard began working in St. Louis while the children and I stayed behind. It was March and school would let out in May. They could finish out the school year while I packed things up to move. Rich drove home, every weekend and his coming was the highlight of our week. We sold the livestock and painted and fixed up the house to sell.

It wasn't very long before Richard found a house and in June, we made the move to Missouri. This was going to be a big adjustment for us. We sold the house in Indiana and began settling in. Connie was 16 years old and Jerry was 15 when they enrolled in their new school. In no time they had made new friends. They came and went with their new friends and seemed too busy for Mom and Dad. I started seeing Wan every chance I got. Sometimes I would spend the entire day with her, while at other times our visit was limited to a quick cup of coffee. It was wonderful having her close to me again.

In June of 1970, Connie graduated from high school. A few months later, she was married to John, her high school sweetheart. My precious little girl was leaving home. As I watched her go down the aisle on her father's arm, my heart swelled with pride. I prayed that life would be good for her. They found an apartment nearby so I was able to see her often.

The following year Jerry finished high school. I felt enormous satisfaction seeing them graduate and thanked God for blessing us with both of them. When summer was over, Jerry went into the military. When he left for basic training in San Antonio, I thought my heart would break.

Thankfully, Connie was nearby. While Rich didn't say much, I could see the sadness in his eyes. I remembered my feelings as a young girl. While love is wonderful, it is also painful.

Connie Meyer, 17

Jerry Meyer, 16

Jerry was married the next year to the young girl who grew up with them in Indiana. She lived on the neighboring farm and spent a lot of time at our house. The three of them spent warm summer nights sleeping in the hayloft of the barn laughing and talking most of the night. As we listened to the talking and giggling, Rich and I decided to play a trick on them. We hid in the barn and made strange noises to frighten them. We laughed as they screamed and tried to figure out what it was. Before long they realized it was us. After much laughing and scolding from them, we promised never to do it again. Now, the three of them were together again, reunited through marriage.

In no time at all, or so it seemed, Connie gave us two grandsons. They were the joy of our lives, and were with us every opportunity that we could manage. As they began to walk and learn what life was all about, we were watching and learning also. John was always Grandpa's boy while Kevin clung to Grandma.

Once when John was walking across the patio, he kept looking fearfully behind him. My first thoughts were that he had seen a snake. Before I could ask him, he cried out "Grandma, what is that thing on the ground that keeps following me?" I laughed as I realized he was seeing his shadow. Those big, blue eyes got wider and bigger as I explained what it was. I could almost see the wheels turning in his little head.

When I was a youngster, there was a popular song played during the war called "Oh, Johnny." As I would sing it to John, his big, blue eyes stared at me intensely. A big smile spread across his face as he listened to every word. When I finished, he applauded loudly. Clapping his little hands together, and beaming brightly, he began to sing to me, saying, "Oh, Grandma." He couldn't know the pleasure he gave me that day.

Kevin, on the other hand, was very serious. He wanted to know everything about everything. He needed to study and touch everything he saw. When we went shopping, I would tell him to "look, but don't touch." Needless to say, this was asking the impossible. His little fingers grabbed everything in sight as he studied it and tried to figure out how it worked.

When I sang to Kevin, I always finished the song with cha, cha, cha. As they rode in the back seat of the car, I would sing to them as I drove. When I finished the song with cha, cha, cha, he would shout grumpily, "No, my song!" as if to exclude John. This, of course, was followed by fighting between the two of them. I tried to ignore them as we drove, but Kevin made sure I heard by shouting loudly Grandmaaaaaa. He stretched the word Grandma out until I was forced to pay attention to him. To this very day, at age 24, he still teases me by stretching out the word Grandma, and believe me, he gets my attention every time. Although they are immensely different, each of them holds a special place in my heart. It would be 10 years before Matthew, our last grandson, would make his appearance.

One day Wan received a phone call from Rudy. He told her that Mom was in the hospital with a blood clot in her leg and the doctors were afraid to amputate it because of her weak heart. They also told him that it would be fatal if the clot traveled to her lungs. Fearing the worst, Rudy suggested that we should come. When Wan told me, I told her to go on, that I would come later. As I studied about it, my thoughts of Mom ran wild. I thought of the many trips I had made because someone thought she was dying. I'm ashamed to tell it, but I even said to Richard "I hope she doesn't ruin our Christmas." It was only a week away. In all honesty, I have to admit that I didn't want to go. A few days later on Dec. 18, 1973, Mom passed away. Wan had arrived too late to see her and I had deliberately stayed away. I am ashamed of this and I ask God and my family to forgive me.

The weather was terrible as we set out for Kentucky. There was 15 inches of snow on the ground and the roads were treacherous. I was dreading to go, but my conscience was driving me on. It took us 12 hours to make a 5-hour trip. When we finally arrived, Wan and Rudy had made all the necessary arrangements. There was more ice than snow in Kentucky, so traveling was even slower as we set out the next morning for Brandenburg, where the funeral would be held.

I approached Mom's coffin with great apprehension. As I stared at her, I felt a flood of emotions which I am loathe to write about. But in order to keep my account factual, I feel I must, in all honesty, tell the complete story of how I felt, and what I did and didn't do. My first thoughts were feelings of sadness. As I looked upon her, my heart cried out to her. "Why could you not love me? Why could you not love your four children?" Next, my thoughts turned to anger. I thought of the orphanage and how the four of us longed for her. I thought of my children and how she couldn't even be a grandmother to them. As I struggled with my feelings, I finally felt a sense of despair. The mom I longed for was gone, and with her, all hopes of loving and being loved were gone as well.

The funeral procession gradually made its way over the slippery roads to St. Theresa's church at Rhodelia. As we sat in the church, I noticed there was very little crying. There was no soft music playing in the background, only silence. I wondered to myself if there was anyone there who loved Mom. We buried her next to her mother, my dear Grandma Hardesty.

When the funeral was over, we returned to Rudy's house to visit with him and Bill before leaving for home. As we sat and talked, my thoughts returned to Mom and Dad. I had wondered if Dad would come to the funeral, not for Mom, but perhaps to comfort us, or give us support. I was disappointed that he didn't come, especially when I saw his brother, Sherman was there. I decided that I would call him and see if he could join us at Rudy's house.

As we talked on the phone, I felt an overwhelming hunger for him. I wanted to touch him and hug him tightly as I had done as a child. I wanted to say I loved him and missed him. When I asked him to come, his reply stunned me. He declined to come, saying that he was getting old and maybe he'd see us the next trip.

Fighting back the tears, I told myself that there wouldn't be a next time. It was still the same old story, not today, maybe tomorrow. I felt like I loved him and hated him all at the same time. I decided I would just forget him, although I knew in my heart I couldn't. He was my daddy.

We left Rudy's house early the next morning. The roads were cleared of snow so the drive was quite pleasant. As we approached our house, we noticed the roads were more snow covered. Being in a rural area, we didn't get the attention that the more populated areas received.

Our driveway sloped downhill, so we approached it very cautiously. One look told us that we couldn't enter it until we shoveled it. We decided to park the car across the road and walk over to the house. Before we could get parked, we heard a car coming over the hill. We could tell by the sound that he was coming too fast to stop, and we knew he was going to hit us. we jumped out of danger just as he crashed into the side of our car.

Now, we really had a problem. We were down to one vehicle and we both had full time jobs. Rich was able to ride to work with a neighbor which enabled me to take the remaining car. This certainly had been a bad week.

Sometime later, Richard and I bought a tombstone for Mom. Uncle Earl had told us that he would set it for us if we would bring it over there. It was a red granite stone with a rose etched in gray on either side of her name and it was very pretty. The four of us, Rudy, Bill and Wan and I shared the cost equally. It was the last thing we could do for our mother.

In the spring of 1974, we received a letter from Owensboro, Kentucky saying our graduating class was having a 25-year reunion and we were invited to come. As I read the letter, I couldn't believe it had been 25 years. I was excited at the thought of seeing all our classmates again. Rich wanted to go with us so we decided we would make a whole weekend of it.

Wan and I decided we would dress alike just for fun. I hoped my first boyfriend, Billy Joe would come. I couldn't wait to see how everyone had changed and reminisce about old times with them. I called way ahead of time to make motel reservations for us. I wanted everything to be perfect for this big event. I wondered if Owensboro had changed much, and would we still remember our way around. I was wild with excitement and I could hardly wait for summer to come.

After what seemed like an eternity, July finally arrived. The three of us, Rich, Wan and I set out early Friday morning so we could spend the day driving around Owensboro. Although it had grown, much of it was still the same. Our old school was gone, but we had no trouble finding where it had been. The town now boasted a hospital and a huge new school which combined several other small schools.

After lunch we set out to find the hall where the reunion was to be held. Although it didn't start until five, we got dressed early. There was no way we were going to miss this affair, and if we got lost, we would have plenty of time to reach our destination. As we drove, we giggled at the things that were still the same, and marveled at the changes that had taken place. There were big new hotels, theaters, and four lane roads. Time had certainly slipped away from us.

When we entered the hall, we shouted with glee. There stood dozens of old classmates, and we hugged every one of them. Some had brought their mates with them, as I had, and some had married fellow classmates. Some came from as far away as New York. There were faces I remembered and names I had forgotten.

There was one girl who I was especially eager to see. Her name was Charlene and she often befriended Wan and me. She occasionally took us to her home to meet her family. When we were lonely and in need of a friend, she was there for us. Although the nuns were good to us, we longed to be with people our own age. We had so much to talk about, fashion, The Hit Parade, and best of all, boys.

Much to my surprise, she was one of the first girls I saw. Unknown to me at that time, she was one of the organizers of the reunion. I should have known! When dinner was finished, there was dancing to the big band music and socializing. We had 25 years of things to talk about. I was disappointed that my high school boyfriend didn't come. When things finally wound down, we left tired, but very happy. Our class reunion is one of my fondest memories.

That same summer Wan and I went to see our brothers. Richard had to work, so we went alone, taking turns with the driving. While at Bill's house, he told us that the boy's orphanage had been torn down and replaced with new homes. We had always wanted to see it one more time, but now it was gone. After discussing it with Bill, we decided we would like to return to St. Vincent's orphanage where we spent our childhood. Bill declined to go but gave us directions so we could go. Fearing that we might not get in, we called and asked for permission.

As Wan talked, I could see the tears come into her eyes as she struggled for control. Sister chided her and told her they didn't like to open the place for visitors. It was now operated as a nursing home and they didn't like to be bothered. Wan explained that it was our home years ago, and that we wouldn't bother anyone. The nun finally relented and told us to come. She would provide us with an escort when we arrived as there were places that were restricted.

After setting up a time, Wan hung up the phone. She buried her head in her arms and began to cry. She told us that the nun was very rude and mean to her. She scolded her as you would a child. She finished by saying that she hated them all. We got in the car and drove straight to the orphanage like two homing pigeons. Even with all it's bad memories, it was still our home. One of the nuns met us at the door and gently pulled us in.

As we stepped in, the first thing we noticed was the absence of the grandfather clock, but there, staring us in the face, was the dinner bell rope which stirred many pleasant memories. We took many a trip from floor to ceiling on that rope. As we went from room to room, we remembered, we laughed and we cried. The nun was quiet as if she understood what we felt.

We ended our tour in the chapel. It was exactly the same as it was 40 years ago. The statues were the same as was the organ which we played at services. We chuckled as we remembered how upset the nuns would get when we hit a sour note. We were only twelve years old then and we made many mistakes as we played. We only played when the organist was ill, so we never became very good at it.

We thanked the nun for her time and went outside. We had taken many pictures of the inside and now we wanted pictures of the outside. We noticed the top story of the orphanage where we had slept years ago had been removed. They had also torn down the janitor's house and the priest's house. The barn, too was gone as was the chicken house where we played.

As we walked around the grounds, we chattered like two young girls. What looked so big to us as children was really quite small. The picnic grounds were covered with trees and brush. The playground, which seemed so big, was now a parking lot. We left feeling jubilant and satisfied. That grumpy nun would never know how happy she had made us. As we exited, Wan found a picture of the orphanage as it is today, laying on the sidewalk. We dusted it off and thought to ourselves what a perfect ending this was to our day. It was as if someone had put it there just for us. I still have that picture tucked away with the rest of my memorabilia.

St. Vincent Orphanage today

We also learned that summer that dear Sister Francis had passed away. Although we corresponded occasionally, I had lost touch with her over the years. Wan, however, had gone to see her several times. I remember her telling me on one occasion, that she had written to Sister Francis telling her that she was coming to see her. When Wan arrived at St. Mary and Elizabeth hospital where Sister Francis was supervisor, she saw her coming down the hall. When Sister Francis saw Wan approaching, she extended her arms and began running towards her. As the tears ran down her cheeks, she grabbed Wan and hugged her tightly, saying "my little girl." I can see this happening in my mind, and I deeply regret I missed it. I see her face and feel her arms around me even as I write this. That dear person loved us so much, even more than our own parents did. I hope with all my heart that she knew how much we loved her too. She was our real mom.

The next time we went to Kentucky, we drove to Nazareth and took a picture of her tombstone. As we stood there in silence, I whispered to her how much I loved her and thanked her for loving us.

CHAPTER VI

In the spring or 1983, Matthew, our third grandson made his appearance. After wishing for a girl for so long, we were a little disappointed at first. But when he smiled at us and wrapped his tiny fingers around ours, we were hooked. He had big brown eyes like his dad, and his mother's smile.

As we watched him grow and begin to crawl, we could see his insatiable curiosity and determination. He also exhibited a great sense of humor which kept us surprised and laughing boisterously.

No sooner did he learn to walk than he began to explore. He got into everything he could reach, and if he couldn't reach it, he pulled over a chair and climbed up on it. His favorite prank was turning the air conditioner up or down. One minute we were freezing and the next, we were ready to melt. When questioned, his favorite reply was "I fixed it."

One summer day, we were sitting out on the patio watching

Matt play with the garden hose. Flashing an evil grin, he pointed it squarely at Grandpa and squeezed the pistol grip as hard as he could. He was squeezing it so hard that his little hands were shaking. When nothing happened, he threw it down, disappointed and confused.

After another unsuccessful try, Grandpa told him that he was pointing the nozzle the wrong way. If he would turn it around, he would be able to squeeze it better with his thumbs. However, unknown to Matthew, this made the nozzle point straight at himself. He turned it around as he was instructed, and, determined to squirt his Grandpa, he squeezed it as hard as he could. This time he was successful. When the water squirted in his face, he threw down the hose, screaming in surprise. Before long, he became angry and tried it again. He was going to squirt his Grandpa regardless of the price.

Once more he picked up the hose and pointing it squarely at his own face, he squeezed the trigger. After receiving another good soaking, he threw the hose down in disgust and returned to his dad. He would tend to Grandpa another time.

It soon became obvious to us that Matthew was going to have a big impact on our lives. While the other two boys were indeed a handful, we could see that Matthew was going to top them both.

Whenever his mother scolded him, he would come to me crying. With his little arms outstretched, and his lower lip quivering, he would cry "my Guumma." and want me to take him. Although I always lifted him up to me, I was careful to reenforce what his mother had said. He and Grandma surely had something special. Was he really that different from his brothers, or were we just getting older?

Ever since we first moved to Missouri, we had been trying to find a place in the country. Now that our family was grown and retirement was not too far away, we began our search in earnest. In January of 1986, we found a 90-acre farm which we liked very much. There were no fences at all and the fields were overgrown with trees and brush. The brush was so tall that many times we had difficulty finding the truck which we had parked in the field.

We made an offer on the farm which the owner accepted. We couldn't wait to get started on fencing and clearing the fields. It turned out to be a much bigger job than we had anticipated, but we were determined to do it.

Thousands of chigger bites later, we got the perimeter fenced. We would tend to cross fences later. We had a well drilled for water, and stayed in a little one room trailer. When the grandchildren came on weekends, they slept in a tent. To say we were roughing it, is putting it mildly.

I cooked on a Coleman stove, and washed dishes in a dishpan. Every morning I filled a wash tub with water and set it out in the sun to heat. That night we took our baths in the wash tub out behind the trees. The one who was the least dirty went first, followed by the other. It wasn't the ideal set up, but it worked.

After the fencing was done, we began clearing trees. While this seemed like an impossible task, we soon began to see the fields.

It didn't take long for us to realize that it was going to be sometime before we could even think of building a house.

As we cleared the land, we were excited at the things we found. There were gooseberries, blackberries, dewberries, hickory nuts, hazel nuts and walnuts. There were wild cherry trees and wild grapes were everywhere. A creek ran through the farm and there were two large ponds. Everything was perfect for what we wanted and we were determined to make it look it's best.

After seven long years of clearing we chose the spot where we would build our house, beneath a hill to break the wind and help us stay warm in the winter. With all the clearing we had done, there was plenty of firewood for heating.

Rich was still working for Chrysler, so our trips to the farm were limited to weekends. It was a little more than 100 miles from our house in Fenton to the farm. I would get food and supplies ready to go, and when Rich came home from work on Friday night, we'd load the truck and set out for the farm. We were too excited to feel tired as we made the two-hour drive. We would arrive at the farm in the wee hours of the morning. After unloading the truck, we usually went right to bed so we could get an early start in the morning.

In late May of that year, our brother Bill informed us that the nursing home had called and said that Dad was near death. As we hurriedly prepared to leave for Kentucky, Wan's youngest son, Raymond, stated that he would like to go along. Raymond had visited his grandpa several times with Wan, and was impressed with him. Raymond was the only one of Wan's or my children who visited Dad during their teen years. All of us had slowly, but surely, lost touch with each other.

I had not seen Dad since 1984, two years earlier. The last time we were in Kentucky, Rudy went with us over to their house to visit. When we talked to Dad, he didn't know who we were. We tried to tell him that we were his children, but he was lost, and unable to remember us. It was heartbreaking to watch him struggle, trying to remember. Daddy had Alzheimer's disease and couldn't remember anything.

Upon arriving at Bill's that evening, we begged him to take us to the nursing home to see Dad. I noticed he seemed reluctant to go, but I brushed it aside, thinking that he was tired. I was so absorbed in my own needs that I never thought that perhaps it was too painful for him to go.

When we entered Dad's room, there, lying on the bed, was this tiny little man. He looked so old and so frail. I remember saying to Bill "This isn't Dad. We're in the wrong room." He replied that it was, but I couldn't believe it. My daddy was big and strong and handsome. This tiny, little man couldn't be my daddy.

I rushed to his bedside, crying out "Daddy, Daddy." I stroked his hair and sobbed like a child. What in the world had happened? Time had played a cruel trick on me. I looked back at Bill. He was sitting there in a chair, his head in his hands. Only then did I realize that I had put him through more pain. Brother Bill was hurting as much as we were.

As Wan and I stroked Daddy and talked to him, he flailed his arms wildly. He was comatose but I am absolutely convinced that he could hear us. He was unable to talk, but I think that by waving his arms, he was telling us that he heard us.

This was our last visit with Dad. We left for home the next day with every intention of returning as soon as possible. That very night, when we got home, Rudy called and told us that Daddy was gone. Upon hearing the news, Wan and I were silent. There were no tears as we tried to absorb the painful news. Finally, almost in unison, we both said "Now, it's finished."

I'm not sure what we were thinking when we said it. Was the longing finished? The searching, the hoping? When the numbness wore off, we realized that it would never be finished. The hatred we had for Evelyn, as well as the jealousy we felt for her children would diminish with time, but we would always remember the good times with Dad before she came into our lives. We would remember that confident stride as he walked up the long walk to the orphanage to see us. We would always hear his husky voice as he talked to us.

We went to Rudy's house the next day. We were all very subdued as Sue, his wife, tried to comfort us and help us. We were not included in the funeral preparations in any way. We waited to hear when and where the funeral would be as any stranger would.

Evelyn eventually called Rudy to tell him when the visitation would be. With this, Wan and I snapped. Hoping to see Dad in private, Wan called the funeral home to see if we could view him before the public arrived. They told us no, that it was up to Mrs. Milam to allow that. Explaining that we were his children, she pleaded with them, but they politely refused.

By now, I was furious. This was my Daddy and I was going to see him. The four of us had things to tell him and we intended to do it privately. I took the phone from Wan and dialed Evelyn's number. When she answered, I just exploded, telling her how we felt and what we wanted. I was determined that this time we would have our way.

After our private viewing, we sat down to reflect and wait for the visitors. We met several of Daddy's friends and many family members whom we had never seen before. As we were sitting there by the coffin, a middle-aged woman came up to us and asked if we were the Milam twins. We told her yes as we wondered who she was. She told us that she was Sister Sheila, one of the nuns who was in Owensboro with us. When we realized who she was, we sprang to our feet and embraced her. In this dreadful time of sorrow, here was someone who brought back good memories of good times. We chatted for a while and then she left.

It was at Dad's funeral that I met my cousin, Kitty and her husband, Bill. Her parents were my Aunt Hettie and Uncle George, who had taken us to their home so many times while we were in the orphanage. Although I couldn't remember Kitty, I resolved to renew our relationship. I had so much family that I did not know.

The next morning, we arrived early at the funeral home for a final visit with Dad. Evelyn and her children were there also, but I deliberately avoided them. As the priest prepared for the final services, Rudy, Bill and Wan and I took a seat in the back of the room with the public.

Suddenly, Rudy sprang to his feet and told the rest of us to come. The four of us defiantly walked down to the very front row and seated ourselves across from Evelyn and her family. "We belong here," he said. "We are his children."

When the time approached for the final viewing procession, the funeral director called Evelyn first and then he beckoned to us. As petty as it sounds, for once, we came first. We, his children, came before his stepchildren. Such a simple gesture by the funeral director did wonders for us.

At the mausoleum, the priest began the final prayers. As I sat there and listened, my heart was breaking and I desperately wanted to cry. On the other hand, I was determined that I wouldn't cry. To keep from crying, I read all the names on the mausoleum walls and fought a terrible battle with myself.

I don't know why I felt as I did. Why did I not want to cry? Was I trying to punish Daddy? Was I trying to say that I didn't care? I have struggled with this for many years, trying to understand myself. Wan told me that she had the same feelings and that she, too, was unable to understand. Were our feelings normal?

We never saw Evelyn or her family again. We never saw the will or learned its contents. We go to Daddy's grave whenever we can to visit with him. This chapter in my life is finished, but Daddy will always be with me. The love-hate relationship I have for him will never die.

After a time, as the pain of our loss was diminished, I was eager to begin a relationship with my cousin, Kitty. She had indicated that she was interested in a family reunion and I couldn't wait to hear more. I had met many family members at the funeral, and even though I didn't know them, I was hungry to know more about them.

Kitty and I began corresponding; and waiting for her letters was pure torture. I devoured every word and saved every letter that I received from her. She answered many of my questions about my family and helped me fill the gaps.

Whenever we went to Kentucky to see my brothers, I managed to see Kitty and Bill as well. I met her sister, Mary, and her brothers who we played with as children. Although I couldn't remember Kitty, I distinctly remembered her brothers. I'm assuming they were nearer our age while Kitty was, perhaps, a little older.

When I first met her brother, Dan, my heart nearly stopped as I stared at him in amazement. He looked so much like Daddy that I could only stare. When he hugged me close, I could barely hold back the tears. I told him how much he looked like Daddy. He hugged me tighter as he told me "You almost became my sisters." Then he told me how Aunt Hettie and Uncle George wanted to take us but were afraid they couldn't provide for us.

That was all I could think of for the rest of the evening. I kept looking at Dan and thinking. I knew I was staring but I couldn't help myself. Daddy would never be gone as long as Dan was alive.

As Kitty and I continued corresponding, she sent me books about Rhodelia, where I was born. She had also researched a genealogy study on our grandparents which she shared with me. As I read and re-read it, I had difficulty keeping the people straight in my mind. I had to read it several times before I could get it right. She also sent me family photos which I tried to connect with the story.

As I eagerly absorbed the story, I realized that at long last, I was learning about my family, who I was, and where I came from. This wonderful group of people was part of my family and at long last, I belonged. Things were finally coming together for me and I owed it all to Kitty. I wondered if she could ever really know what she had done for me.

We resumed our weekend trips to the farm. We drove down every Friday evening and returned on Sunday. Although we were making lots of headway, there was still much work to be done. Someday this piece of land would look like a real farm.

In early May, Connie told us that her husband, an Air Force man, was being sent to England for a year. All the soldiers were required to put in time on foreign soil and he had chosen England for their tour of duty.

They would drive to New York where they would board a military plane for Europe. Their car would come later on a ship. While I understood that they had to go, I couldn't imagine what life would be like without them.

Connie had always lived nearby and we had a very good relationship. I never thought the time might come when she wouldn't be near me. We spent a lot of time together, shopping and doing those mother-daughter things that people do.

The boys also spent a lot of time with us. We had many good times together, and they were a wonderful help to us. In fact, the year we bought the farm they were with us the entire summer. They helped us cut trees and clear the fields. Their youthful energy kept us going when we wanted to quit.

It was going to be a big adjustment for us. With Connie and the boys gone, it was as if part of our lives had suddenly ended. We corresponded often and called each other weekly. We thought of all the little things we were going to miss. No more loud fighting from the bigger boys and Matthew wasn't around always fixing things.

In January of the following year I decided to go see them. Being terrified of flying, I was afraid to go, but I needed to see my family. They had been gone for seven months, and I longed to see them. Rich was working a lot of overtime and was unable to go with me, so I asked Wan if she would like to go. When she agreed, I was elated and we immediately began thinking of all the things we would need for the trip.

We went shopping for some new clothes, got a new perm, and excitedly made the necessary preparations. There was so much to do and so little time to do it in. I tried to plan ahead for Richard's needs while we were away, and took care of any business matters that I could for him.

About a week before we were to leave, I was helping Richard carry firewood. I was trying to stack it neatly in a row when I dropped a big log. As it landed on end, the other end hit me right in the face. In just a few hours, I had the prettiest black eye that I had ever seen.

I hoped it would be gone before our trip, but it wasn't. It just got purple and blacker, and more swollen. I knew I was just going to have to live with it, and endure the stares that were sure to follow.

Richard drove us to the airport the morning that we were to leave. When I approached the ticket agent for my ticket, he smiled broadly as he stared at my black eye. I feel sure he thought that I was running from someone and fleeing to Europe. I chuckled to myself as I realized that I was going to see a lot of staring as people jumped to their own conclusions. There was one person who actually winked at me.

When we boarded the plane, I immediately buckled my seat belt and never moved out of my seat. I refused to drink anything fearing that I might need to go to the bathroom. While the other people watched the movie, I looked out the window. It was an eight-hour flight so sleep was inevitable. I managed to doze, but remained upright in my seat with my seat belt fastened.

Wan, however, loved flying and was very relaxed. She talked and did her best to distract me. She had been to Europe before and was excited about going again. As frightened as I was, I was on my way to see Connie and the boys in England.

We landed early the next morning around six o'clock. Before we went to customs, I wanted to use the bathroom. Unable to find one, I asked a lady to direct me. She pointed to a small room marked "water closet", their name for the bathroom.

After freshening up, we took the elevator, or "lift", as it's called in England, down to customs. There we lined up for questioning. When the customs agent asked Wan why she was in England, she told him she was visiting her niece who lived there. Next he asked her where her niece lived. Not knowing the address, Wan looked toward me, and with a giggle, replied "I don't know."

As the agent looked my way, he abruptly stopped talking and stared openly at my eye. I tried to maintain my composure as he stared, but despite my efforts, a big smile spread across my face. I knew what he was thinking as he stared at me, and I tried to stifle the giggle that I knew was coming. With a disapproving look, he resumed looking through his papers.

I can't imagine what the agent thought, but the look on his face was priceless as he looked from one of us to the other. Finally, with a disdainful look, he motioned us through. Still giggling, we headed for the lobby where we could see Connie waiting. I am confident the customs agent thought we had been drinking.

We stayed a week with Connie and had a wonderful visit. We toured an abandoned castle which looked just like the ones you saw in books. It was made of gray stone, with narrow winding staircases. We also saw houses with thatched roofs, and open food markets where vendors sold their wares. The fields were thick with green, and so lush that you wanted to lie down in them. It was a beautiful country indeed.

In October of 1988, we lost Richard's dad. He was 80 years old and died peacefully in his sleep at home. We traveled to Indiana for the funeral and returned home three days later. Richard's mom was a very strong individual, and would be all right. Richard's four siblings lived near her and would look after her.

The following December we received the most painful and shocking news ever. on Dec. 18, the same day that Mom had died, Wan's middle son, Eddie died of a heart attack. He fell over dead while he was cutting firewood. Being only 30 years old, it was simply unbelievable to us.

When Wan told me on the phone, I just couldn't absorb it. As she screamed hysterically that Eddie had died, I just kept asking "Eddie who?" When it finally registered, I knew I had to go to her. Rich and I got in the car and left for her house. She lived about 25 miles away, but it seemed like an eternity to get there. As I hugged her and tried to comfort her, I felt completely helpless. How could I help? What could I do? She just sat in the chair as if in a daze, while her children tried to comfort her.

Realizing that she would have lots of company to feed, I decided to go home and cook a meal for her and her family. I baked a ham and made several cold dishes that she could easily serve. I also made some pies for them to snack on when they got home late. As she thanked me, I cried for her, my beloved twin sister. While she grieved for her son, I grieved for her.

Richard was pall bearer at Eddie's funeral. Afraid to leave Wan, I stayed at her side every moment. To see her so heartbroken was a devastating experience. Wan and I went to Eddie's grave many times. I listened patiently as she went over the details again and again. I knew that in time it would get easier for her, but until it did, I would be there for her, to listen and to comfort her.

We were together a great deal for the next few months. Although we both worked, we found time to be together, to talk, and to cry. Before long, things began to get better. Wan still talked about Eddie, but now, she spoke of the memories, his youth, and the good times. At last, time was easing the pain.

CHAPTER VII

In no time at all, it was 1990. Richard had worked for Chrysler for 30 years and was beginning to think of retirement. Although he was only 58, he was eligible for retirement after 30 years with the company. I hadn't worked for several years but I, too, was eager for him to retire.

There were so many things we wanted to do, and retirement would give us the opportunity. We were eager to build a house at the farm, but weekends just didn't give us enough time to do it.

In July, Richard was offered early retirement with a good pension and paid health insurance. To say we were excited is an understatement. We were like two kids in a candy store. While Richard worked on plans for a house, my thoughts were of livestock and gardening. Now, we could stay at the farm as long as we wished.

We hired a contractor to lay the foundation for our house.

When he was finished, our work would begin. We would build the house ourselves, in our own time. It wasn't long before we had floor joists built, and the walls framed. It was beginning to look like a house! When the time came to put up the rafters, we knew we would need help. I was too short to be of much help to Richard.

Jerry and his wife, Sandy came to our rescue. And of course, dear Wan was always there, doing anything she could to help us. While the three of them hung rafters, Wan and I insulated under the floor. I never knew there was so much to be done. When the outside was finished, we stood back and surveyed our work. We had done it! The walls were finished on the outside, and we were ready to begin work on the inside.

Richard and Jerry had spent a great deal of time working on the floor plan. We decided to have only 2 bedrooms, but they would be large rooms. We bought unfinished cabinets for the kitchen, and we would stain them when we finished painting the walls.

I chose a soft gray color for the walls. It was easy on the eyes and was different from the white that most people used. As I worked and worked, I began to think that the more I painted, the more there was for me to paint. After two coats of primer and two coats of gray, I was finally finished with the walls.

Next, I began working on the kitchen cabinets. Since they were made of oak, I decided to finish them in a clear urethane in order to enhance the natural beauty of the wood. We had cabinets laying all over the house and in every room. I rubbed them with steel wool between each coat to ensure a smooth finish.

With Wan helping me, we finally finished them. They were absolutely beautiful.

When the time came to think of carpeting, Richard and I decided to drive to Georgia, where most of the carpeting is made. We felt that we would have a limitless selection, as well as varying degrees of quality. We also learned that if we had it shipped to Missouri, we wouldn't have to pay the Georgia sales tax. The cost of shipping was equal to the amount of sales tax.

We chose a soft blue color which I thought would complement the gray walls. We bought enough to carpet the entire house except for the kitchen. I couldn't wait for it to arrive. For the kitchen, I selected a unique pattern of linoleum. It was comprised of tan and brick-red cobblestones scattered randomly on a beige background. When I first looked at it, I didn't care for it, but the longer I looked at it, the better I liked it.

I told myself as I studied it, that it wouldn't show dirt and would hide spills and spots. As we laid it on the floor, I felt quite proud of myself. But it wasn't long before I began to wonder if I had made a good choice. My pride changed to frustration as I realized that it not only hid spots, it hid everything that fell on it, from beans to coins. The only way I could find what I had dropped was to crawl around and run my hands across the floor. It seemed this time, I had gotten more than I bargained for.

No one could have been prouder than Richard and I. Slowly, but surely, our house was coming together and we had done it all ourselves, with a lot of help from our family.

In 1995, our oldest grandson, John, announced that he was getting married. The wedding would take place in October, giving us several months to prepare for it. It was going to be a big wedding, with a reception, followed by dinner and dancing. While we were happy for him, we found ourselves wondering how this could be. Was he really old enough to get married? Where had the time gone?

As we pondered these questions, we realized that time had slipped away from us. Our two oldest grandsons had become young men. At the same time, our own children were middle aged. How could this be possible?

Not long after the wedding, John and his new bride moved to Atlanta, Georgia. Although we hated to see them go, we understood that they had to make their own way, wherever they chose to do it. As it turned out, Atlanta was a good choice. It was the same distance to his wife's family in Florida as it was to John's in St. Louis.

The next year, on Jan. 10, we lost Richard's mother. She was only sick for a few weeks before she passed away, so it came as a real shock to all of us. Although she was 83, she was active and alert and, as always, jovial and loving.

Richard and I always drove to Indiana to see her at least once every three months She was always glad to see us and made us feel most welcome. On the last trip we made to see her, she told us that she felt terrible. Not being one to complain, we knew there was something wrong with Grandma. After staying with her for the weekend, we returned home to Missouri.

A few days later, Richard's brother, Alan, called saying that they had admitted Grandma to the hospital, where she was diagnosed with lung cancer. We wanted to return immediately, but there was a big snow on the ground, which forced us to postpone it. Before we could return, Grandma was gone. In just two weeks, dear Grandma had passed away. We were shocked and heartbroken as we prepared to return for the funeral. Richard and I truly loved her as a friend as well as mother and mother-in-law.

The crowd was enormous at the funeral service. In the many years I knew her, I never, not once, met anyone who disliked her. She was the kind of person who made everyone like her immediately. She was warm and loving, and while I am proud to have known her, I am even prouder that she was my mother-in-law. As we greeted her friends and family, we cried with them and marveled at her accomplishments. To be loved so much by so many is indeed a great legacy.

That same year, we received an invitation to Bill and Kitty's golden wedding anniversary celebration. It was being held in Kentucky with a family get-together and dinner. I was so excited I could hardly wait. We had attended several gatherings with Kitty and her siblings which we thoroughly enjoyed. Some were like family reunions where we visited and became acquainted with each other's children.

But this one was special. We were celebrating 50 years of marriage, of disappointments, and accomplishments. And what an accomplishment this was! I was so happy for them I thought my heart would burst.

As we looked at the pictures of Bill and Kitty on the walls, and read the story of their life, I could almost see it happening. There were pictures of them in their youth with small children, as well as later pictures which depicted their accomplishments. They had much to be proud of indeed.

As the D. J. played their favorite songs, everyone danced and drank champagne. I met their three children and their grandchildren. Their son, John, had married a girl from Missouri, who was from a small town near us. Of course, there was plenty for us to talk about.

Their daughter, Paula, was an absolute delight. She was bubbly and friendly, and a pleasure to be with. We didn't get to see much of their daughter, Ellen, but I hope to get to know her better in the future.

Much too soon, the party was over. What a wonderful day it had been! All the family were gathered together and Wan and I were right in the middle of it. I was dizzy with happiness as I looked at all those wonderful people. Here, gathered around me, was my family!

Bill and Kitty's anniversary party was a great success. As we bid them goodbye, I told myself how lucky I was. I not only had a family; I had a loving family. What more could one want?

Later that year, we finished moving all our belongings to the farm. Finally, we could call it home. We had gradually moved our things over a period of time, so there wasn't much left to bring.

Now, I set about decorating the house, and thinking of a garden. I loved gardening, and was most eager to get started on it. The next spring, I planted everything I could think of. I canned vegetables and froze vegetables. I had cantaloupe coming out of everywhere. Finally, I gave them to anyone who would take them, and plowed the rest of them under. I told myself, that next year, I would restrain myself.

I made blackberry jelly and wild grape jelly, as well as numerous gooseberry pies. I froze what I couldn't use for next year. Most of the time there were plenty of berries for picking, but, occasionally, in a dry year, there weren't any to pick. At these times, I had berries in my freezer for jelly.

We fertilized the fields and sowed them in clover. We mended cross fences and made driveways through the creek so we could cross at will. Now, finally, it was starting to look like a real farm.

The following spring, we bought a few head of cattle. They were mainly feeder calves, which we would sell in the fall. They proved to be one of our best investments, not so much for what they would bring us in cash, but for what they did for the farm.

As I mentioned earlier, a small creek ran across the farm. It was so overgrown with brush and weeds that you could hardly find it. As the summer got hotter, the cattle gathered in the creek for water. They bedded down in the brush to hide from the sun and rubbed on the trees to scratch the flies from their backs. As they tumbled around fighting flies, they soon crushed all the brush and briars.

When the sun went down in the evening, they slowly ventured out to graze. Before long, the creek banks looked like a park. There were paths running through them, and hardly any brush was standing. In searching for relief, the cattle had done us a great favor.

Although the cattle are a lot of work and worry, Richard and I both enjoy them tremendously. As you study them, you learn that they are just like people. While some are friendly, others are timid. Some are demanding while others beg. They talk with their eyes, sometimes begging and questioning, and at other times, threatening, when necessary.

They know their owners and come to greet them. They show their affection with gentle rubbing, and soft licks of their tongue. In time, we came to love them as other people loved their pets.

Before we knew it, the years had slipped away. We were so busy that we didn't notice that we had gotten old. Richard was 66 and I was 67. Suddenly, we had become senior citizens! Although we have slowed down somewhat, we still work on the farm and continue to enjoy it.

As I look back at the years, I am filled with emotion and gratitude. It has been a good life, with much satisfaction. Richard and I have had many good years of true happiness together. In the troubled years, when I first met him, he was my savior and my hope. Today, he is my rod and my staff. My love for him grows stronger every day, as he fills my life with happiness.

Although the young years of my life were painful, I look back on them and try to understand them. While I feel indifference towards my mother, I have loving and pleasant thoughts of Daddy. I know in my heart that he loved the four of us or he couldn't have come to the orphanage so many times. I still remember sitting on his knee and I can hear him call us "Snookums". How truly sad that time, miles and Evelyn drove Daddy and us apart.

When I think of my brothers, I feel a great tenderness for them. Brother Bill is my buddy who I can joke and laugh with. When we were small, Wan and I used to put bobby pins in his hair. He never complained as we fussed over him. I can see him yet, with his blonde hair pinned back, just smiling at us. I wonder if he knows how dear he is to us, and how very much we love him.

Dear Brother Rudy was always the authority figure in our lives. We looked at him in awe and saw him not only as our brother, but as a father figure as well. Wan and I were crazy about him, but there was always that feeling of reservation that any child has for his parent. As unfair as it is to Rudy, I still have that feeling. When family matters arise, I instinctively look to him for answers. In all those childhood years, dear Brother Rudy was our big brother and daddy too. As I have told him numerous times, "My brother, Rudy, is the best brother in the whole world." The four of us, without any parents, and separated as children, have a special bond between us. We stood alone, fought life's battles alone, and we survived.

Over the years, I learned many things about my grandparents from Kitty and other family members. Dear Grandma Hardesty, who always looked so sad, did, in fact, have an unhappy life. Her first husband, my Grandpa, was 24 years her senior. When he died in 1931, almost a year before I was born, she was only 51 years old. In time, she remarried. Her son, my Uncle Earl, told me that her new husband wasn't good to her and didn't treat her kindly. He never elaborated on this and I didn't feel free to ask questions.

When I first met her in 1951, Grandma had no electricity in her home. She ate her dinner by kerosene lamps. When she died in 1957, she still didn't have electricity or running water. I never met her second husband. He was never around when we were there. No wonder dear Grandma had such sad eyes. Life, it seems, wasn't very kind to her. She was widowed young and was lonely in her later life.

I also learned much about my Grandma Milam. She was Kitty's Grandma as well as mine and she had much to tell me as I pleaded for news of the family. I also needed to understand why Grandma was so cold when we first met her. I hoped Kitty could give me the answer.

Grandma Milam had a hard life also. When she married my Grandfather, he was 30 years older than her and was the same age as her own Father. She told Kitty how he used to read poetry to her. Grandpa had grown children from a previous marriage, some of whom, were the same age as Grandma Milam. In time, they had 8 children. Grandma worked hard on the farm, plowing the garden with a walking plow and working like a man. Most of the work fell on her shoulders due to an injury Grandpa received while fighting in the Civil War. He was unable to work much and complained of constant pain.

She, like my other Grandma, was widowed young. There were

My Paternal Grandparents

still young children at home and she would have to provide for them. She applied for, and received widow's benefits from his pension. While it wasn't much, it would help. I don't know how she provided for them, or herself. She had four wild, young sons who were almost more than she could manage.

I learned also from Kitty, that Grandma was nearly deaf. Perhaps that explains why she appeared so cold when I first met her. Maybe she never heard anything that was said. On the other hand, why did she not ask us to be seated or to come in? I told myself that Grandma was so worn out that nothing mattered anymore. She was too old and too tired to care.

Eventually, I traveled to Rhodelia and found the cemetery where most of my family are buried. As I gazed at their tombstones, I uttered a sigh of relief as I finally felt a sense of closure. While I never knew most of my family, I was content with what I had learned about them. These people were my family, and I loved them all.

One day I took a long walk down in the field as I often did. I loved the peace and solitude as I gazed at the trees and watched the various wildlife. As I sat beneath a tree, I thought of my family and my life. It was at this time I decided to write this story. My life, I thought was worth writing about. Having been reared in an orphanage was not unique during those times. It was the depression era and many people were needy and unable to provide for themselves.

What I find astounding is how the nuns could take in someone else's children and teach them and nurture them. While there was never any emotional contact from the nuns, they taught us good moral values, they educated us, and provided for us. They also taught us how to cook, sew, and play the piano.

Although a few of them were mean, the majority of them were kind, if not loving. I can still see them fighting for self-control as we deliberately and cruelly taunted them and defied them. Unhappy with our situation in life, we vented our anger and frustration on them, the very people who cared enough to care for us.

I have to ask myself what I would have done had the roles been reversed. How would I have handled all those unhappy youngsters? In all honesty, I have to admit I would have thrown up my hands in despair. Instead, they tolerated us and cared for us. With humility and gratitude, I thank them from the bottom of my heart.

The more I look back at my life, the more I realize that I have much to be thankful for. I was blessed with a loving husband, two delightful children, and three grandsons. Although Mom and Dad were never a part of my life, I have two wonderful brothers who love me and best of all, I have dear Wan, my beloved twin sister.

I have enjoyed 49 years of marriage and have raised my children successfully. While to some, this may be no great accomplishment, it was my goal in life. I was never interested in a career. All I wanted was to be a good wife and mother. Since my mother was never part of my life, I had no role model or mentor. I worked out my problems on my own, as best I could. I mothered my children by instinct rather than knowledge. Neither of my parents ever knew how many children we had.

Frankly, I believe I have achieved my goals. I pursued my dream, I lived it, and I did it all, no thanks to Mom and Dad.

My story would not be complete without this final comment. That dreadful oatmeal mush that I hated as a child, and threw behind the steam radiator when the nuns weren't looking, is now, ironically, a big part of our breakfast diet. Richard loves it and in fairness to him, I serve it at least, twice a week. I still shudder as I eat it. While the bowl no longer seems as large as it did then, it still contains that dreadful oatmeal mush.

THE END

CPSIA information can be obtained
at www.ICGtesting.com
Printed in the USA
LVHW080303160723
752386LV00010B/880

9 781977 218766